GLADIOLI
AND THE MINIATURES

GLADIOLI AND THE MINIATURES

ROY GENDERS

THE GARDEN BOOK CLUB
121 CHARING CROSS ROAD
LONDON W.C.2

First published 1961

Blandford Press Limited
16 West Central Street, London, W.C.1

Printed in Great Britain by Fletcher & Son Ltd., Norwich

CONTENTS

Part I

v

CONTENTS

Part II

LIST OF PHOTOGRAPHS

ACKNOWLEDGMENTS

Acknowledgment, with grateful thanks, is made to John Gledhill for Figs 5-16 which he took in conjunction with the author; to G. F. Gardner for Figs 1-4; to Konijnenberg & Mark for Figs 17-22; to Jack Fisher for Fig 23; to Dobbie & Co. Ltd., (Edinburgh), for Figs 24 and 26; and to W. J. Unwin Ltd., for Figs 25, 27 and 28. We are also indebted to Mr Frank W. Unwin for his help on the Classification of the of the Gladiolus and on the Primulinus Section of Part II.

PART I

❧ I ❧

The Gladiolus
– An Introduction

HALF A CENTURY AGO, a writer had this to say of the gladiolus: 'We have to acknowledge that it can hardly be classed as one of the great flowers of the people.' What may have been true fifty years ago is far from being so today for the gladiolus is now one of the most popular flowers of the garden. Indeed, the Dutch bulb growers have stated that they now sell more gladiolus corms each season than all the autumn planting bulbs together.

The popularity of the gladiolus may be due to its being of such easy culture and to the fact that it is not too particular as to soil, requiring little by way of fertilisers. It is also entirely labour saving, requiring no disbudding, whilst the small flowered types will not even need support, and with its upright habit the gladiolus is a most suitable plant for the small modern garden. Being in bloom during the latter weeks of summer and throughout autumn, a time when the full beauty of most of the summer flowering perennials is coming to an end, the rich colouring of the blooms will bring a new beauty to the garden equalled only by that of the dahlia.

The gladiolus is also one of the most attractive of all flowers for indoor decoration, large numbers being grown for this purpose each year by specialist cut flower growers.

The gladiolus may be grown almost anywhere in Britain, though in the colder climate of the north the later flowering varieties should be omitted. Those who garden south of a line drawn from the Mersey to the Humber will find that even the later flowering varieties will open in time to provide several weeks of colour in the garden before autumn has ended. The modern gladiolus is sufficiently hardy for it to be grown as far north as the Shetland Isles, provided those varieties are planted which come early into bloom.

Its Introduction to Britain

The gladiolus is not by any means a plant of recent introduction though it has only latterly become popular. Gerard, in his *Historie of Plantes* (1597), mentions two European species G. *communis* and G. *segetum*, whilst Parkinson in his *Paradisus* (1629) illustrates and describes G. *byzantinus*, the Corn Flag of Constantinople, so called because its strap-like leaves resembled those of the flag iris. The plant was introduced to this country from Turkey and an illustration in the *Paradisus* shows it as having six tubular shaped blooms to each stem one above another, the blooms pointing in the same direction. They are of rich red colouring, and there is also a pure white form, *albus*. Parkinson mentions that this species bloomed later than the others, during August, and it would appear to have been much used in early crossing for of all the then known species it most resembles the gladiolus of today. Sir Thomas Hanmer, whose quite recently published manuscript was written just three centuries ago, was the first to mention a South African species. This was G. *aethiopica* which also had bright red flowers. From the beginning of the eighteenth century, South African species were introduced in quick succession and were used by hybridists throughout the world to raise new hybrid varieties.

The scarlet flowered G. *brenchleyensis* was the first important introduction to be made in Britain. The famous French hybridiser, Victor Lemoine, crossed it with G. *purpurea-auratus* and produced a race with beautiful butterfly markings on the petals. This he called G. *lemoinii* which, crossed with seedlings of the scarlet flowered G. *saundersonii*, produced the G. *childsii* section, named after John Lewis Childs, an American who purchased the complete stock. It was an American, Arthur Kunderd, who in 1907 introduced the first gladiolus with the attractive ruffled petals we now know so well.

Another species which was to play a large part in the raising of the modern gladiolus was G. *cardinalis*, its bright scarlet blooms having a central white blotch. Crossed with G. *spittacinus* by Monsieur Bedinghous, it produced the famous Ghent gladiolus, G. *ghendavensis* or G. *gandvensis*, which had striking scarlet and yellow blooms. G. *cardinalis* when crossed with G. *tristis*, which has scented flowers of cream with red markings, and comes into bloom early in July, produced the distinct G. *colvillei* section which bears its flowers during the early weeks of summer. It is usually grown under glass or outdoors in the most sheltered gardens in the south-west.

Small-Flowered Gladioli: The Primulinus

Though the colour range had become most interesting by the beginning of the present century, it was not until the early years of the century that a number of introductions were to bring an entirely new popularity to the gladiolus. In 1904, Fox who was then working on the erection of a bridge across the Zambesi River at the Victoria Falls, discovered growing in the mist created by the falling water, an entirely new form of gladiolus of great beauty. The blooms were more dainty than any species previously known whilst the stamens were protected from the spray by an attractive hooded petal. Blooms were first exhibited at the Royal Horticultural Society in 1906 and G. *primulinus*, with blooms of clear primrose-yellow, quickly became a favourite. The hybridists soon took it up, especially James Kelway of Langport and W. J. Unwin of Histon, who at the same time was working on the sweet pea. Unwin found that G. *primulinus* produced a range of entirely new and distinct colours as well as retaining the attractive hooded petal. The firm have since won every honour for these gladioli.

The Primulinus gladioli have smooth edged petals, the blooms having three outer petals of almost triangular form. The top inner petal is large and folds over at the top whilst the small lower petals are slightly reflexed. The blooms are spaced out along the stem in ladder fashion, there being more space between the individual blooms than with the large-flowered varieties thus giving a lighter, more dainty effect to the flower stem.

The Butterfly Type

Another form of the small-flowered gladioli is the Butterfly type, introduced by Konijnenburg & Mark, Holland. Like the Primulinus, they grow about $2\frac{1}{2}$–3 ft tall, the individual blooms being only about half the size of the large flowered gladiolus. Whilst the petals are slightly ruffled, their beauty lies in the attractive throat markings which gives the blooms the appearance of exotic butterflies. A form, with greater ruffling of the petals, has recently been introduced by Mr Leo Klein in Canada where Mr Leonard Butt introduced his now famous Ruffled Miniatures. The plants grow nearly 3 ft tall, the heavily ruffled florets being under $2\frac{1}{2}$ in. across and have the appearance of orchids.

The Miniatures

The Ruffled Miniatures, in spite of their name, are slightly larger in all respects than those of the Primulinus type but are smaller and more dainty than the large-flowered varieties. They may be said to bridge the gap between the Prims and their larger sisters and with their ruffled petals have a gaiety not to be found in other forms.

In America, Fischer has given us a Miniature with ruffled petals, but which has the floret placement of the Primulinus, and which may become an entirely new section. The true Miniature which grows less than 12 in. tall may not be so far away. Indeed, we already have the species G. *mostertiae* with its deep pink flowers and G. *cuspidatus* which bears white and purple flaked blooms. Both flower in May and on only 6 in. stems. If crossed with both the Primulinus and Miniature forms they may breed a plant suitable for the smallest of gardens and one which blooms particularly early. Unfortunately most of the dwarf species suitable for breeding are early summer flowering and as the corms are somewhat tender, it is not always practical to plant them in autumn to remain in the open ground during winter, as is necessary with gladiolus intended for early blooming. In time, hybridisers may, however, be able to overcome this difficulty.

Scented Gladioli

It is now possible to report a new race of Purbeck Scented hybrids which have been evolved by Capt. Barnard in Dorset. They are miniatures with scented blooms and flower early in summer. They are best grown under glass. From the U.S.A. comes a fragrant large-flowered gladiolus named Acacia, for it has the perfume of mimosa (*Acacia dealbata*). Thus the gladiolus is on the point of taking on a new popularity and soon the exquisite fragrance of G. *tristis* may have become prominent in all groups.

❧ 2 ❧

The Gladiolus in the Border

GIVEN GOOD CULTIVATION, each spike is capable of bearing two dozen florets, the modern varieties opening 8 or more florets together in attractive double-row formation. The florets are often 6 in. across.

With a flowering period of at least three months, where early, mid-season and late flowering varieties have been planted and growing to heights varying between 2–3 ft, the modern gladiolus is an excellent plant for the border. A border may be made up entirely of gladioli, or form part of the herbaceous border.

In the herbaceous border the corms may be planted at least two weeks earlier than usual, for they receive the protection from cold winds provided by the young foliage of other border plants. This will enable the very early-flowering varieties such as 'Appleblossom', 'Aranjuez' and 'Show Girl' to come into bloom by mid-July, when the main border display provided by the lupins, delphiniums and pyrethrums will have come to an end.

With their upright habit and occupying only a limited amount of ground, the gladioli may be planted in spaces about the border resulting from plants dying back during winter, or near plants which have made only a limited amount of growth. Gladioli may be used in the same way as annuals, planting early in April each year and lifting the corms when the border is made tidy early in November.

The corms should be set out in circles or groups of five of each variety to provide a liberal splash of colour. About 8 in. should be allowed between each corm.

The gladioli will provide the same brilliance of colouring as the dahlia and will bloom at the same time, but whereas the dahlia makes a large bushy plant and requires plenty of room in

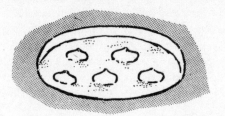

the border to develop, often obliterating nearby plants, the gladiolus is of neat, upright habit and does not overlap. It will not exhaust the ground to anything like the same extent as will the dahlia.

The large-flowered gladioli will require staking to support the heavy weight of bloom, and border plants growing nearby will help to hide the stakes until the gladioli can partially do so when they come into bloom.

Corms may also be planted in a shrubbery, provided plant growth is not so dense as to deprive the gladioli of sunlight and moisture. The corms may be planted about low-growing shrubs and will appreciate the protection which they will provide in early summer, when cold winds may cut back the young gladioli foliage. Advantage may be taken of this by planting earlier than usual.

A Gladioli Border

Where a border is entirely of gladioli, plant groups of the taller flowering varieties at the back, with the less robust to the centre and groups of the miniature and Primulinus types in the front. Those large-flowering gladioli of the most robust habit and suitable for planting at the back of a border are:

Annie Amelia (M)—Cream
Appleblossom (VE)—Pale pink
Bermuda (ML)—Salmon-pink
Blue Goddess (EM)—Purple and blue
Bow Bells (VE)—Pink and buff
Caribbean (E)—Blue
Chamouny (M)—Cerise-pink
Chinook (ML)—Salmon
Eiffel Tower (M)—Lavender-pink
Flower Song (E)—Deep yellow

Heirloom (M)—Lavender
Innocence (EM)—White
Jack Fallu (M)—Brown-red
King Size (ML)—Salmon-pink
Landmark (M)—Creamy-white
Mid-America (M)—Light red
Pharaoh (M)—Salmon-pink
Poppy Day (EM)—Scarlet
Roberta Russell (E)—Fiery scarlet
Victory Day (E)—Cerise-pink
Winston Churchill (M)—Red

From this group a selection may be made not only to provide a wide variety of colour but also a succession of bloom over as long a period as possible.

Where planting in a border to themselves, a strip of ground about 3 ft wide should be chosen, facing south so that the plants will obtain all the sun they require and preferably in a position where the plants will receive protection from strong winds by means of a wall or overlap fencing.

Planting

Plant in groups of 4–6 corms, working in the colours so that they will not clash with each other and planting so that there will be as few spaces about the border as possible. To provide a long succession of colour, plant early, mid-season and, where conditions are favourable, late varieties.

In planting these groups approximately 1 sq ft of soil should be removed to a depth of 6 in. where the soil is light and sandy, or to a depth of 4 in. where it is of a heavy nature. The sand or peat is spread over the soil to a depth of about 1 in., into which the gladioli corms are pressed. The soil is then filled in and made level again. This is a better method than planting by means of a trowel, for it is possible to ensure that all parts of the base of the corm are in contact with whatever material is used for their planting.

To keep the flower spike as tidy as possible, the lower florets which are the first to open should be carefully removed as the blooms begin to fade. This will enable the beauty of the top florets to be enjoyed without the distraction of faded blooms appearing on the stem at the same time.

Flowering Times

The following large-flowering gladioli will come early into bloom:

Abu Hassan	June Day (VE)
Adoration	Little Pansy
American Express (VE)	Manchu
Anna Mae (VE)	Mandalay
Appleblossom (VE)	Maria Goretti
Aranjuez (VE)	Maytime
Bengalen	Myrna Fay (VE)
Bow Bells (VE)	Orange King
Cardinal de Jong	Paul Rubens
Caribbean	Pink Lustre
Caswallown	Ravel
Dr Fleming	Roberta Russell
Flower Song	Show Girl (VE)
Friendship (VE)	Southern Belle
Gold Dust	Spun Gold (VE)
Golden Show	Storm Cloud (VE)
Greenland	Tahoe (VE)
Huntress	Tosto
Jean Golding	Victory Day

Those varieties marked (VE) come first into bloom and are especially useful for garden display and the early shows.

There are also a number of varieties which may be classed as second-early flowering and which will bridge the gap between the early and mid-season varieties:

Artist	Pactolus
Blue Goddess	Phantom Beauty
Dutch Beauty	Poppy Day
Innocence	Redowa
Memorial Day	Royal Stewart
Merry Widow	Sequin
Moonlight Glow	Sparkler
Mother Fischer	Spic and Span
Niels Bohr	Tabarin
Ninety Grand	White Goddess

These varieties are amongst the most outstanding of all gladioli both for exhibition and garden display.

Those who garden in a cold climate should guard against planting the late flowering varieties and particularly those which come into bloom the last of all. In suitable districts where the corms may be planted earlier, they are extremely useful for extending the season, often until well into October.

These large-flowering gladioli bloom late:

Albion (VL)	Mrs J. McKelvie
Andrena	Ogarita
Boise Belle	Oklahoma
Burma	Picardy
Catherine Beath	Pinnacle
Cover Girl	Princess Beatrix (VL)
Eureka	R.B.
Evangeline	Salman's Sensation
Flying Fortress	Sieglinde
Grand Monarch	Swiss Flag
Henri de Greeve	Toekana
Lorelei	Tunia's Wizard
Mighty Monarch	White Challenge (VL)

FIG 1—When planting gladioli in the border, the holes should be made with a trowel—about 4 inches deep.

FIG 2—Planting in a trench with the corms on sand to assist drainage.

FIG 3—Efficient staking and tying of the Large-flowered gladioli is essential.

Fig 4—The second tie, made a week or ten days later.

Fig 5—Lifting the plants in autumn, when the foliage has begun to die back.

Fig 6—Gladioli plants laid out on ground after lifting to dry.

⫸ 3 ⫷

Large-flowering and Miniature Gladioli for Bedding

～～～～～～～～～～～～～～～～～～～～

THE GLADIOLUS IS A suitable plant for bedding, its tall upright habit relieving the flat appearance of a bed which may be filled with more dwarf summer bedding plants. Particularly arresting is the display provided by a round bed containing the dwarf yellow cactus dahlia 'Downham', and planted among them orange, scarlet or purple gladioli which provide contrast in colour and height. If both early and mid-season varieties are planted, there will be a brilliant display during the latter weeks of summer and well into autumn.

The modern dwarf bedding dahlias are valuable as they come into bloom soon after they have been planted out in early June, and by early July they will be a mass of colour. Advantage should be taken of modern early-flowering gladioli of compact habit to plant with them. 'Anna Mae', with its dainty pure white blooms, is lovely used as a contrast to the dwarf dahlia, 'Pride of Edentown', whilst 'Little Pansy' is most attractive where planted with 'Jean Thompson', with its blooms of cherry-pink.

The miniature gladioli are ideal for planting with dwarf dahlias, and may also be used with dwarf flowering annuals. A display of great brilliance is to be obtained where antirrhinums are used in contrasting colours to the gladioli.

One of the most striking displays seen by the author was of a long, rectangular bed filled with white antirrhinums amongst which had been planted glowing scarlet gladioli 9 in. apart.

Equally attractive is the pink antirrhinum, 'Malmaison', with the miniature gladiolus 'Wedgewood' whose lavender-pink flowers with their cream coloured throats provide a delightful combination with the pink antirrhinums. Where the pale yellow miniature 'Statuette' is grown with a bed of scarlet petunias, the plants reach their full beauty together.

Also in bloom at the same time as the gladioli are the asters, the pompones with their bushy, branching habit making a colourful display during the latter weeks of summer and throughout autumn. Extremely colourful is 'Pirette', the large button-like flowers being of vivid scarlet cerise with a large white centre. A most colourful display is to be obtained by planting them amongst a bed of Primulinus gladioli of various shades of yellow.

As an alternative, make up a bed of dwarf marigolds 'Helen Chapman' and 'Lemondrop', both bearing vivid golden blooms on 6 in. stems and the miniature gladiolus 'Red Button', with its blooms of brilliant scarlet. There are many other colour combinations equally attractive.

Small-flowering gladioli are charming used with dwarf early flowering perennials. Beds made up with modern strains of the polyanthus to bloom throughout spring and with sweet williams to continue the display until the gladioli takes over towards the end of July, will provide colour from March (if polyanthus 'Barrowby Gem' is planted) until September. Edge the bed with winter flowering violas to provide colour throughout the year and for a more brilliant display in spring and early summer, plant tulips which may be left in the ground for two years. All the attention the bed will require will be to lift the gladioli in October each year and to replant with new corms in April.

The dainty Primulinus forms are most attractive where growing amongst beds of pansies and violas. The new 'Clear Crystal' strain of pansies, bearing flowers of very bright, clear colouring, and free from the usual pansy markings, make a pleasing ground for the dainty gladioli, whilst the free flowering violas 'Bullion' and 'Bluestone' are also delightful in this way. You can plant blue lobelia and white alyssum amongst plants of gladioli, when the foliage appears in May. The half-hardy annuals will quickly form dense clumps to completely cover the ground. Here, the gladioli should be planted 9 in. apart, using yellow and scarlet varieties for contrasting colouring, and if the Miniatures or Primulinus forms are used, there will be no necessity to stake.

When the gladioli have finished flowering, the attractive sheaf of sword-like leaves of glossy green will provide an added attraction to a bed of summer flowering plants for several weeks after the dead gladioli blooms have been removed. The leaves, with their bronzy colouring, are also attractive as they make growth early in summer.

Selecting a Situation

Wherever gladioli are to be grown, they must be given a sunny position. Being natives of South Africa and the shores of the Mediterranean, they will not tolerate shade in any way. Indeed, in a wet, sunless summer they will rarely be seen at their best. They may be planted against a wall or against a background of wattle hurdles to protect from the wind, but they should never be deprived of sunshine. Wherever possible, corms should be planted where they may receive the maximum amount of sunshine. This is especially important for the later flowering varieties, for by September the strength of the sun's rays and the hours of sunshine diminish day by day and the blooms may not open if not growing in a sunny position.

Never plant gladioli beneath trees or where the plants will receive shade from the overhanging eaves of a house, for they will grow up drawn and weakly with the stems unable to support the bloom. Even the partial shade of tall trees will deprive the plants of the necessary sunlight. There are numerous plants that will grow well under such conditions so that the sunniest positions about the garden may be available for the gladioli. Care should also be taken to guard against draughts which will retard the plant from coming into bloom, even though it may be growing in a sunny position. Cold conditions and planting into a badly prepared soil will not only delay flowering but may bring about the introduction of numerous diseases through a weakening of the vitality of the plant.

Protecting the Plants

Protection from strong winds is essential if the flower spikes are not to grow bent especially where large-flowering varieties are concerned, whilst strong winds may cause damage to the petals of the florets and spoil their appearance.

My own gladioli beds are protected by 5 ft wattle hurdles against the strong east winds which blow directly off the North Sea. The beds face due west so that the plants obtain the maximum amount of sunshine from just before noon until the late evening. Hurdles prove more satisfactory than a hedge to give protection, for most hedging plants are gross feeders, depriving the gladioli of moisture and food in the soil. Where the ground is exposed some protection from strong winds must be provided. Such protection will also prove valuable during the early weeks of summer when the young foliage will be appearing above the ground and may be troubled by the cold winds of May.

⇘ 4 ⇙

Preparation of the Soil

〰〰〰〰〰〰〰〰〰〰〰〰〰〰〰〰〰〰〰〰

WITH ITS GREAT BEAUTY of form and bearing individual blooms of enormous size and substance, the modern gladioli is without rival both as an exhibitor's flower and for garden display. Indeed, it is of such magnificent appearance where grown well that it is worthy of giving detailed culture whether the bloom is to be exhibited on the show bench or enjoyed in the garden and in the home. And no plant will respond better to being given that little extra care in its culture.

Functions of the Corm

The gladiolus has what may be called a double rooting system. As soon as the corm is planted, fibrous roots appear from around the circular mark at the base. It is these short, fibrous roots which sustain the corm in its early days until a new set of thick, fleshy roots appear, not from the base but from the top of the corm where the buds had appeared. These roots feed the flower spike and build up the new corm, which forms at the base of the flower stem on top of the original corm. As the season advances, the fibrous roots of the old corm will be replaced by the vigorous new roots which search down to a considerable depth for moisture and food. Where a flower spike of exhibition quality is required, it will be necessary to give the ground a thorough preparation, working the soil to a depth of two 'spits' when sufficient humus materials and plant food should be incorporated to provide both for the building up of the new corm and for the formation of a flower spike of enormous size.

To grow a large spike of exhibition quality, the gladiolus will require ample supplies of moisture and sufficient plant food to last until the corm is lifted in autumn. This means that whatever the condition of the soil considerable quantities of humus must be provided together with those materials which release their plant foods slowly and over as long a period as possible. Artificial fertilisers of inorganic form should not be used, apart from a little sulphate of potash to accentuate the colour of the florets. Nor must the corm be permitted to come into contact with rank manure in any form, for this would cause it to decay.

Humus and Plant Food

Though gladioli are not too particular as to soil, producing quite good spikes in a heavy soil as well as in one of a light, sandy nature, the better condition the soil is brought into the greater will be the chance of obtaining first rate flower spikes. That the soil should be well drained is of first importance, actually requiring greater attention than the provision of plant food. Stagnant water remaining for long periods about the roots will cause decaying of the corm through insufficient root action, whilst the appearance of the flower spike will be delayed even if the corm has been able to survive. Again, where there is a badly drained soil, the corms will be difficult to clean and dry when lifted in autumn and there will be numerous losses during storage.

Lucky indeed is the gardener who has at his command a friable loam, for it should require little by way of plant food and will usually be well drained. Mostly, however, the soil will contain either an excess of clay particles or too much sand. In the one case it will be necessary to open up the clay particles to assist drainage; in the other, it will be essential to provide humus to retain moisture. A light soil will also require larger quantities of plant food. The gladiolus enjoys a neutral soil, so where there is a high lime content this may be neutralised by the addition of

peat. The acid soil of a town garden on the other hand will benefit from a liberal dressing of lime which in its caustic (unhydrated) form and used on a heavy soil will open up the clay
particles.

The most suitable time to prepare the ground, and especially a
heavy soil, for gladioli is in the autumn. A clay soil will then
obtain the benefit of the winter frosts whilst light land will have
time to consolidate after humus materials have been incorporated. If unhydrated or caustic lime is dug into the soil in
October, the action of the moisture in the soil will act on the
lime causing it to break up just as if a mild volcanic eruption
had taken place. This will cause the clay particles to disintegrate,
so bringing the soil into a more friable condition and greatly
assisting drainage. If the soil is left in a rough condition over
winter, the action of wind and frost will cause further dis-
integration, and by spring, a heavy clay soil will be in a more
suitable condition for planting gladioli corms.

Lime will also play an additional part in the preparation of
the soil as it will enable it to release its plant foods which, in a
soil that has not previously been worked, will have been stored
up through the years. As the clay particles become disintegrated,
this will permit oxygen in the atmosphere to set in motion bac-
terial activity, again making it possible for the humus manures
to become converted into food readily assimilated by the plants.
Soil which 'pans' during periods of prolonged rain and drought
will prevent this activity and the plants will suffer in consequence, obtaining little benefit from the materials provided.
The lime will also correct any acid tendency which may be
caused by deposits of soot and sulphur where the garden is
situated in or near a town.

When the soil is ready for working, which will possibly be
towards the end of March (or autumn in the case of a light,
sandy soil), as much humus as possible should be incorporated
whatever the condition of the soil.

This may take the form of composted straw, peat, shoddy, bark fibre, seaweed, hops or farmyard manure. For those living near the coast, seaweed or fish waste should be obtained. Gardeners in the north will find shoddy readily obtainable, whilst used hops will be available from most breweries. All are rich in plant food in various forms and are easily handled, being in no way offensive. Peat, too, which is devoid of actual plant food but which is a most valuable source of humus, is also inexpensively and readily obtainable. Each of these fertilisers may be conveniently stored for use when required and is an excellent substitute for farmyard manure which, for the townsman, is difficult both to obtain and to store. Nor must we neglect the compost heap, where damp straw may be composted with an activator and where lawn mowings and partially decayed vegetable matter, including leaves, may be added throughout the year to decompose into a compost suitable for digging into all types of soil. Where farmyard manure is to be used, it must be thoroughly decayed. For preference use well-rotted cow manure and, as with all the humus forming materials and plant foods, see that it is dug well into the soil, to a depth of at least two 'spits' or about 18 in. Remember that the new roots go down to at least this distance in search of food.

Where peat or bark fibre is to be used to provide humus, then organic manures should be used in addition. These fertilisers should be those slow to release their food and a balanced diet should be provided containing nitrogen, phosphorus and potash. Nitrogen will build up a vigorous plant and a large corm for the following season; phosphorus will stimulate root action and will help to form new roots, whilst potash will improve the quality of the bloom. Bone meal, containing both nitrogen and phosphorus, may be used at the rate of 2 oz per square yard and this is dug in as the soil is prepared. The potash may be given 2 oz per square yard dressing at planting time and this is merely raked into the surface. Or wood ash (stored dry) may be given as a liberal dressing at the same time. As an alternative to the bone meal, hoof and horn meal, also containing both nitrogen and phosphorus may be used, whilst steamed bone flour (best used in spring) should be used in conjunction with dried blood. The following table showing the food values of the various organic fertilisers may provide some assistance in the preparation of the soil:

Fertiliser	Action	Nitrogen content %	Phosphate content %	Potash content %
Farmyard manure	Slow	0·5	0·25	0·5
Fish meal	Quick	10	8	7
Guano	Quick	15	10	5
Bone meal	Slow	5	20	—
Poultry manure	Quick	3	2	6
Seaweed	Slow	0·4	—	1·5
Hop manure	Slow	4	2	—
Shoddy	Slow	12	—	—
Dried blood	Medium	10	—	—
Steamed bone flour	Slow	1	27	—
Feathers	Slow	8	—	—
Wood ash	Quick	—	—	10
Sewage sludge	Slow	1	1	—
Hoof and horn meal	Slow	10	10	—

Heavy soils will retain ample deposits of the chief plant foods though these will not be released in the form in which they are readily assimilated by the plants unless lime is present in the soil. Light, sandy soils will always be hungry soils, plant food being readily washed away, thus making it necessary to replenish with humus and fertilisers almost continuously if satisfactory results are to be obtained.

Here again, organic manures, which will release their plant food more slowly than will artificial manures, should be used where possible.

Chalk land will present a problem during dry warm weather, for there will almost always be only a shallow depth of top soil. This will cause the soil to become hot and dry as it becomes baked by the sun. In consequence, the plants will dry out at the roots and may die back altogether. With such a soil, it is important to increase the depth of top soil as much as possible and the quickest and most efficient method is by 'green' manuring. Rape seed is sown in August and when it has grown about 6 in. tall it is dug in as deeply as possible. The dense mat of root growth will form valuable humus, whilst the 'green' will supply both humus and plant food. This may be augmented in early spring with composted garden material or by any of the humus-forming manures described which will enable the soil to retain moisture and will keep the plant roots cool during warm periods.

Chalk or limestone land will require no additional lime, but a dressing of peat may be given from time to time to help to neutralise the alkalinity.

Preparing the Ground

The work should always be done by thoroughly digging the ground rather than by employing a mechanically propelled implement, for as the manure and humus is dug in, all perennial weeds should be eradicated. It is also important to dig as deeply as possible—'double digging' or 'trenching', as it is called—so that the ground is prepared to the limit of the plant's root run. This will encourage deep rooting, and a vigorous root system means a healthy vigorous plant.

The ground should be dug at least two 'spits' deep, a 'spit' being 9–10 in. To trench the ground, soil to the width of the spade and about 18 in. deep should first be removed. Manure or humus-forming materials to provide drainage and aeration is placed at the bottom of the trench, over which is-placed soil dug from the next width of ground and enriched with organic manure. Thus the work continues until the whole area has been trenched, and in the final trench, the soil which was removed from the original trench is replaced. The ground will then be prepared to a depth of at least 18 in. With land lying over a chalk subsoil, the top soil may only permit trenching to a depth of 12 in. or even less, though 'green' manuring will increase the depth of top soil.

Where the ground is of an extremely heavy nature, and tends to be low lying, 'walls' of straw, placed in an upright position between each trench, will help to open up the soil and assist drainage. As the straw will tend to use up available supplies of nitrogen in the ground, materials rich in nitrogen should be provided, though a liberal dressing of lime will release any available nitrogen.

It is most important to remove all perennial weeds such as couch grass, nettles, docks and buttercups which will otherwise compete with the garden plants and rob them of their food. They will be much more difficult to eradicate later.

Further Conditioning of the Soil

More may yet be done to bring the soil to a state of thorough preparation and one of the most valuable materials of modern times is vermiculite. This is a mica preparation, obtained from ore which is mined in South Africa and subjected to temperatures of over 2,000° F. The material is, of course, sterilised and is quite clean and light to handle. Gladioli love to get their roots into the golden grains and some amazing results have been achieved. It is as yet quite expensive and though excellent for breaking up heavy clay soil, a more economical use of vermiculite is to plant in trenches 2–3 ft wide. A layer of vermiculite should be placed in the trench at planting time, over which the corms are planted. The soil should have been prepared in the usual way.

Particularly should a trench be used for growing gladioli where the land is heavy and possibly low lying. Soil to a depth of nearly 2 ft should be removed to the required width and into the bottom a layer of boiler ash or shingle should be placed. Then should follow a layer of thoroughly decayed manure, shoddy, hop manure or material from the compost heap over which is placed soil which has been previously brought to a fine tilth as described. As the soil is replaced, more decayed manure or other slow-acting organic fertilisers should be mixed in, together with some peat or bark fibre. The trench should be filled in so that it is slightly higher than the surrounding ground and should be made rounded at the top so that heavy rain may drain away more readily. Where the ground is low lying it may be advisable to dig a small trench around the bed into which surplus moisture may drain.

Whilst the soil is being made ready it should also be treated for pests, particularly wireworms which will attack the young fibrous roots of newly planted corms. Treat the soil with Vaporite plus Aldrin, a powder which is shaken into the soil as the ground is prepared. As the preparation contains naphthalene, it should be used in autumn or at least a month before planting so that any obnoxious fumes may escape. A 1 lb dressing should be used to treat 25 sq yds of ground.

By whatever method the ground has been prepared, it should be allowed at least several weeks to consolidate before any planting is done.

≫ 5 ≪

Bringing the Plants into Bloom

〰〰〰〰〰〰〰〰〰〰〰〰〰〰〰〰〰〰

WHERE GROWING SPIKES OF exhibition quality, a top size corm should be planted, one between 12–14 cm in size which will be almost 2 in. in diameter. For garden display, a 10–12 cm size corm will be suitable, but guard against planting cheap corms which may be of doubtful quality. The corms should have a high crown and should be plump rather than thin and shallow. Corms which are soft when pressed or are hollow at the top should never be planted. The most vigorous corms are those which have more recently been grown from the spawn or tiny cormlets which are to be found clustered around the base of a mature corm. A young corm grown in this way may be expected to give a finer flower spike than those raised from corm to corm over a period of many years. Such corms will often have become acclimatised to the type of soil in which they have spent their life. Where facilities are available, the exhibitor will enjoy the best results where cormlets are obtained and grown on to a corm of 12 cm size. The process of growing on the corm-lets, which is described in a later chapter, will, however, take at least three years before the corm is capable of producing a bloom of exhibition quality.

For an extra early crop, though the gladiolus will not with-stand transplanting when once it has formed its root run, the corms may be started into growth in boxes of peat in the same way as begonias or potatoes. By sprouting very early flowering varieties, it is possible to have them in bloom by the first days of July in the south and by the middle of the month elsewhere.

A greenhouse, cold frame or the window of a warm room

will prove suitable for sprouting, the corms being placed in shallow trays containing a layer of peat which is kept slightly moist. The corms should not, however, be started until between 2–3 weeks before they are due to be planted out. For southern gardeners this will mean starting the corms around mid-March for planting out early in April, for the corms must have only just begun to sprout and must not have made more than the minimum of root growth when planted out.

Planting Times

For bloom of exhibition quality no more than one bud to produce the flower spike should be allowed to remain. Any others must be carefully rubbed out. Where growing for garden display, then a large-size corm may be allowed to grow two or three flower spikes.

Where growing for exhibition it is necessary to plant only those varieties which will open several florets at the same time, at least six being necessary for a spike to gain an award. For garden display, it is preferable if the florets open at intervals, for this will prolong the display.

The last days of March in the more favoured districts, where the soil has been well prepared and is in a friable condition, or the first days of April will be early enough for the first plantings. The corms must never be planted if the soil is wet and sticky following snow, frost or heavy rain. Where the soil is of a clay texture, planting will best be delayed a few days until it has had time to become warmed by the sun's rays. There is nothing to be gained by planting too early in a soil that is still wet and cold.

Planting the very early, mid-season and late flowering varieties will ensure a continuation of bloom from early July until early October. The late flowering varieties, however, should be omitted from northerly gardens as the blooms would not reach perfection in time for the late summer shows. A succession of bloom may also be obtained by planting early flowering varieties over a period of five or six weeks, making one planting each week beginning at the end of March.

Planting the Corms

As the earlier flowering varieties will take approximately 90 days to reach perfection in southern gardens, the mid-season varieties taking 100 days and the late varieties about 120 days, it is possible to calculate the correct time for planting from the various show dates. To make quite certain of having a number of spikes in perfect condition at the correct time, it will be advisable to spread out the planting over a period of about a week or ten days whilst the state of the soil must also be taken into consideration with the planting programme. Again, to be sure of having sufficient spikes of a variety of outstanding quality on show day, at least six corms of each of the selected varieties should be planted. Preference should be given to certain colours for flowering at certain times. For example, many of the white, cream and yellow varieties bloom early, so do the purple and smoky varieties, whilst the dark reds and many of the pinks bloom late, though in each section there are of course exceptions. Northern growers should omit the late flowering varieties and concentrate on the early and mid-season varieties. Even the early flowering varieties in the north will take a fortnight longer to come into bloom than in the south. This means that it will be well into August before the mid-season varieties come into bloom from a mid-April planting and they will thus be right for the late shows.

To guard against thrip, before planting, place the corms in a paper bag containing some DDT and shake them well up.

Whether or not specially prepared beds have been made up or whether the whole area of ground has been brought into suitable cultivation, the best method of planting where bloom of exhibition quality is required is to take out a trench 5–6 in. deep where the soil is light and sandy or 3–4 in. deep where the soil is heavy and the ground possibly low lying. A thin layer of peat, sand or vermiculite should be placed at the bottom, using peat for light land, and into this the corms are gently pressed. Too shallow planting in light land will mean that even the small-flowered types will require adequate staking at an early date.

To grow the large-flowered exhibition gladioli at least 6 in. must be allowed between each corm and preferably 8 in., for the new roots will require all the food and moisture they are able to obtain. My own method is to take out a trench 4 ins. deep, for my soil is of a medium loam, and rather more than 2 ft wide. This will allow four rows 6 in. apart to be planted in the prepared bed but the corms are allowed 6–8 in. between each other in the rows. Where space is available the bed may be made nearly 3 ft wide, allowing nearly 8 in. between the rows. In any case, to allow the roots greater freedom before they come into contact with neighbouring corms, it is advisable to stagger the planting.

The ground between the corms may thus be hoed diagonally. It should be said that no more than 5–6 in. need be allowed between corms of the small-flowered types.

Between the beds, a path 18 in. wide should be allowed, from which the gladioli in the beds are tended.

After the trench has been planted, a covering of peat should be placed over and around the corms before the trench is filled in, taking care to round off the surface to enable rain water to drain away readily if the soil is heavy or the ground low lying.

Into the replacement soil should be mixed a quantity of wood ash or 1 oz per square yard of sulphate of potash, given at planting time.

Guard against planting too deeply. A depth of 3–4 in. is sufficient for heavy soil and an inch or so deeper where the soil is of a sandy nature. It must, however, be remembered that the deeper the corm is planted, the more will it be able to support itself when coming into bloom. Too shallow planting will mean that even the Primulinus varieties will require supporting at an early date, and the foliage may appear above the ground whilst late spring frosts are still present and become damaged.

Care after Planting

Nothing should be done, apart from accurate naming of the corms, until the leaves have grown about 6 in. high which will take about three weeks. From then onwards dusting with DDT powder every ten days until the florets are about to open will prevent an outbreak of thrip which will cause the flower petals to turn brown at the edges besides damaging the corms. If the weather continues dry during May, it will be necessary to soak the ground thoroughly, possibly every third day and in the evening. Never at any time should the plants be allowed to become dry at the roots, and when the flower spike has formed larger quantities of water will be needed not only to bring as many florets as possible into bloom at the same time but so that the flower spike will remain fresh for several days when cut. At this time, the newly formed corm will also require copious supplies of moisture to make the maximum amount of growth. The new corm begins to form when the plant has been growing for a month and has formed three leaves. By then it will be about 9 in. high.

The hoe should then be taken between the plants regularly, making sure that it does not come so near to the corms as to cause damage. Keep the soil constantly stirred and remove any perennial weeds by hand, again taking care not to disturb the corm, for if the roots are made loose, the plant will die back.

At this stage, the plants will benefit from a top dressing which will help to conserve moisture in the soil and to suppress annual weeds. It will also provide the plants with extra nourishment as the flower spike begins to form. Peat mixed with some thoroughly decayed cow manure, or a mixture of soil and used hops will prove of value, the bed being covered to a depth of nearly an inch. Earthing up of the plants may be done and this will provide support at an early stage in their growth.

Feeding the Plants

After about eight weeks when the plant has formed five or six leaves, it will be possible to feel the embryo flower spike by gently pressing the sheaf of leaves near the base. A hardness will denote that the spike is on its way and the plant must be given copious amounts of moisture, watering the ground to saturation point every day if necessary. Liquid feeding should also begin at this stage. This should consist of alternative applications of dilute manure water and soot water given once a week. The proprietary brand of Liquinure in diluted form will be more readily used than where dissolving a bag of animal manure in a tank of water. Soot water, however, is best made up in this way. Liquid feeding should be done during showery weather, whilst during dry weather it is best given immediately before the ground is to be given a soaking. In this way the plant food is washed down to the roots before it can evaporate. For the same reason, the ground should be given a thorough soaking when the sun has gone down, for if the moisture does not penetrate to the roots they will turn towards the surface in search of it. Lack of moisture will mean a shorter flower spike and florets lacking substance, whilst the new corm will not fully develop. As this is of the utmost importance the feeding should be continued almost until it is time for lifting the corm and long after the flower spike has been removed or has died. To prevent a wastage a ring should be made in the soil around the plant and about 3 in. from the stem and into this the manure water is poured.

As the season advances lawn mowings or peat should be spread out over the bed to conserve moisture.

Staking

The large-flowering varieties will require staking and especially where growing exhibition quality bloom, when a slightly bent or twisted spike may spoil what otherwise would be one of outstanding form, staking must be efficient. It must be remembered that with the modern gladiolus the spikes often grow 5 ft tall and will carry up to two dozen flower buds half of which will be open together. Those who have seen the flowers after heavy rain will realise just how great a weight the stem has to support. It is in fact almost impossible to do this unaided and each stem should be given an individual stake. This may be a strong cane 6 ft in length or stout stake which should be inserted well into the ground about 2 in. away from the base of the stem so that it will not injure the corm. The stake should be of sufficient length so that it may support the whole length of the flower stem.

The stake should not be inserted until the buds have formed and it can be seen which way the florets will face. This may be determined by noticing which way the end of the spike is bending and inserting the cane behind it. The spike should be fastened to the stake in three places at regular intervals from near the base. Use wide fresh raffiia so that it will not cut into the stem and make it quite secure so that the petals cannot rub against the stem during windy weather.

Where the corms have been planted in the border as a square or circle, no more than three stakes (or canes) placed at regular intervals between the foliage will be necessary to provide adequate support. This will enable strong green garden twine to be looped around each flower stem and to the stakes, thus disposing of the need to use individual stakes for each stem.

❧ 6 ❧

The Bloom for Exhibition and Indoor Decoration

‹∞∞∞∞∞∞∞∞∞∞∞∞∞∞∞∞∞∞∞∞∞›

THE GLADIOLUS IN ALL its forms is one of the most satis-
fying of flowers for exhibiting, for it is doubtful if any other
flower can reveal such beauty on a single stem. With modern
varieties as many as a dozen florets, often almost 6 in. in diameter will be open at the same time to give the appearance of a
sheaf of orchids.

There are usually Classes for exhibiting gladioli at local
shows. The International shows arranged by the Royal Horticultural Society and by the British Gladiolus Society are open to
entries from all parts of the world. The schedule of the British
Gladiolus Society contains almost a hundred Classes for entry
and covers every conceivable type of gladiolus from the Midget-
flowered to the Giant-flowered.

Show Requirements

For show purposes, the gladiolus is divided into three main
sections:

I. *Grandiflorus*. This covers all sections except the true
Primulinus and Primulinus Grandiflorus groups.

(a) Midget-flowered. The florets not to exceed $1\frac{1}{2}$ in. in
diameter.

(b) Miniature-flowered. Here the florets must be more
than $1\frac{1}{2}$ in. but not exceeding $2\frac{1}{2}$ in. in diameter.

(c) Small-flowered. In this group, the florets to be over
$2\frac{1}{2}$ in. but not exceeding 4 in. in diameter.

45

(d) Medium-flowered. The florets to be over 4 in. but not exceeding 5 in. in diameter.

(e) Large-flowered. The florets to be over 5 in. in diameter but not exceeding 6 in.

(f) Giant-flowered. The florets to be over 6 in. in diameter.

II. *Primulinus*. The florets to be hooded and not exceeding 3 in. in diameter, and carried on slender stems.

III. *Primulinus grandiflorus*. The florets to be hooded and 3 in. in diameter, and loosely arranged on wiry stems.

For consideration by the judges for the awarding of points the spike should be fresh and straight with both the blooms and foliage free from blemishes. The flower spike should be long and unbranched and still have the lower floret attached. The more open florets on a stem, the more meritorious will the spike be. The florets should be regularly spaced and with all but the two Primulinus sections, they should completely hide the stem. The blooms should narrow gradually from the base to the top; they should be of pleasing form and of good texture and colour.

A spike which is bent or has a drooping tip which will give it a lifeless appearance, or which carries old or blemished flowers will never be considered for maximum points. Neither will a short spike nor one with too few open florets. For old florets which are fading and dying the judges are empowered to deduct 3 points for each defective bloom. If two florets have been removed, 2 points will be deducted for the first and 3 points for the second. Petals which are unduly thin or lacking colour or have blemishes caused by pest, disease or the weather, will also be penalised. Richly coloured blooms of good substance will only be provided by good cultivation from the beginning which means a soil enriched with the necessary plant foods. Other points in the correct presentation of the spikes will depend upon such details as staking; encouraging the florets to face the same direction; shading and the artistic presentation of the bloom.

As we have seen, careful staking is important in the presentation of a straight spike. It is also important to have the florets facing the same direction and in this they may require some help. After the spike has been staked the lower buds should be gently pressed in the direction in which it is desired that they should open. Thus the florets will not only open in the same direction but will be so placed as to hide the stem, whilst there will be no overcrowding if the buds are spaced out correctly. With most of the modern gladioli and with many of the older varieties, assistance in this matter is not necessary but with some, if not given help, the appearance of what would otherwise be an outstanding flower spike will be spoilt by badly placed florets.

To achieve success on the show bench a large-flowered gladiolus must be capable of opening at least 6 florets at the same time and with some varieties as many as a dozen will be possible. These exhibition varieties will open 10 florets or more at the same time:

Athlone	Mrs R. Errey
Bow Bells	Noweta Rose
Cecily Anne	Phantom Beauty
Chinook	Pinnacle
Cotillion	Polynesia
Dr Fleming	Snow Velvet
Evangeline	Spic and Span
Firebrand	Strathnaver
Mid-America	Sunspot
Moonlight Glow	Tahoe

For exhibition purposes, the ideal would appear to be a flower spike 24 in. in length, with 8 florets fully open, 8 more showing colour and 8 in bud, evenly spaced along the stem in a double row.

During dry, sunny weather, unless the first florets to open are shaded, they may have lost their freshness and much of their colour by the time some of the upper florets have fully opened.

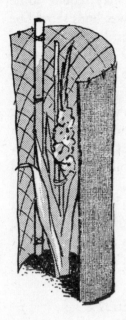

An efficient method of providing shading is to fasten a length of wire netting about 2 ft wide and 3 ft long to a stout stake which is driven into the ground immediately behind the supporting cane. The netting is then bent round the bloom and as the first or lower florets begin to open a piece of muslin or clean sacking is fixed across and around the wire so that the open florets are shielded from the direct rays of the sun.

Cutting the Bloom

One method is to cut the spike as soon as the first florets begin to open. This will prevent the bloom from being soiled by rain and if the stem is placed in a bucket of cold water in a cool room where the light is diffused, six or more florets will open during the next three days whilst the lower florets will still remain fresh. The bloom should be cut as low as possible, but to preserve the vitality of the new corm at least five or preferably six leaves should be allowed to remain on the plant so that the sap is able to drain back into the corm to provide valuable nutriment. To remove more leaves will be to seriously weaken the corm and an inferior spike will be produced the following season.

Cut the stem immediately above the junction of the fifth leaf which will be about 12 in. above soil level. Use a sharp knife so that the leaves will not be bruised and unnecessary leaves will not be pulled away when the bloom is cut. The lower 12 in. of stem should be immersed in water and if a deep bucket is used the rim will support the bloom. Care must be taken to ensure that the blooms do not touch the side of the bucket as the buds open.

If the bloom is cut about four days before the date of the show with the lower florets just opening, the spike should have reached perfection on show day. Approximately three months should be allowed for an early flowering variety to open fully from a mid-April planting where growing in the south. The mid-season varieties growing in Britain in the Midlands will take another three weeks and an additional week where growing in the north.

Transporting the Bloom

To transport spikes of the modern large-flowered gladioli, which often measure up to 4 ft in length when cut, calls for some care. Some growers transport the blooms in large upright crates, but it will be found that the petals will not be in any way damaged if the spikes are placed flat in long wooden boxes, made about 12 in. longer than those boxes used to transport quality bloom to the wholesale markets. The box should first be lined with clean sulphite paper over which the spikes are placed with the florets upwards. The double row of open blooms will occupy considerable space and no more than three or four blooms of exhibition quality should be placed side by side in a box 2 ft wide. The spikes are held in place by canes covered with sulphite paper to form a cushion. One is placed across the box just beneath the lower florets and another lower down the stem. If the cane is made quite firm it will prevent the blooms from making undue movement. The box may also be made sufficiently deep so that one or more trays may be placed above each other, so that one box will accommodate a dozen selected spikes.

The flower spikes should be unpacked carefully so as not to damage the petals and they should be placed without delay into buckets of water. As much of the stem as possible should be immersed, but make sure that the lower florets do not come into direct contact with the water. Give the spikes as long a drink as possible, then place them in the vases so that the blooms face in the same direction. The modern gladioli with its double row of 8–10 blooms will provide a striking display. Artificial supports are not allowed but titivating the florets, so that placement of the blooms will be as near perfect as possible, may be done prior to the judging.

When the spikes have been placed in the vases, they should be wedged in position so that the considerable weight of bloom does not cause them to flop about. Wedging may be done by using small pieces of the stem which should be removed when placing the spikes in the vases so that they will be of similar height and to enable them to take up water more readily. And do not forget to name your exhibit.

Indoor Decoration

Remaining fresh when cut and placed in water for at least a fortnight, under reasonable conditions, no flower is more suitable for indoor arrangement than the gladioli. The blooms do not drop their petals, whilst the spikes will open their florets when in water so enabling the beauty of the blooms to be enjoyed from the time the petals begin to unfold. If the spikes are cut when the lower florets are just on the point of showing colour, they will remain colourful for fully a fortnight. The lower florets can be removed with scissors as they fade and the upper florets begin to open, thus disturbing the arrangement of the spikes as little as possible.

Certain varieties will open their florets when in water very much better than others and these varieties should be given preference where growing chiefly for cut flower purposes. Again, a number of the large flowering gladioli bear a more dainty spike than others; in particular may be mentioned 'Hokus-Pokus', 'Little Pansy', 'Friendship', 'Anna Mae',

'Myrna Fay', 'Adoration', 'American Express' and 'Blue Smoke', the florets being small in comparison with such varieties as 'Leeuwenhorst' and 'Picardy'.

Those large-flowering varieties with attractively ruffled petals should also be grown for cutting together with the ruffled miniatures which are so delightful for flower arrangement. 'Blue Smoke', 'Bow Bells', 'Dieppe', 'Edith Elliott' and 'Geoff. Wightman' bear florets of medium size with beautifully ruffled petals.

But perhaps the most valuable of all varieties are those bearing flowers of pastel colourings for they seem to mix well with almost any variety. 'Phantom Beauty', bearing flowers of a glorious shade of pastel pink; 'Southern Belle', with its florets of smoky pink with a blue sheen; and 'Storm Cloud', its smoky salmon blooms having a splash of gold in the throat are of such shades as to be quite unknown amongst gladioli colourings until more recent times.

Arranging the Bloom

A large earthenware vase will be ideal for the large-flowered varieties. If painted black it will enhance the display where the vivid scarlet and yellow varieties are used. A large vase of green glass will also be most suitable, but as the stems of the spikes will be thick, the container must have sufficient room at the top to allow for as many as a dozen spikes if the arrangement is to be seen to advantage. If the spikes are cut when just showing colour this will not only ensure the fresh appearance of the bloom, but will enable a more artistic arrangement to be made. Heavy spikes with as many as ten huge florets open together may look right on the show bench, but will never make for a pleasing display in the home. How much more attractive will be those long, graceful spikes with the lower florets just opening, whilst the display may be enhanced by using the Butterfly and Miniature forms.

To relieve any stiff appearance of the blooms, sprays of Golden Rod and *Aster luteus* may be used. Both have masses of tiny yellowish-green flowers so arranged on the stems as to present a dainty, feathery habit. Another member of the Aster family which is so useful for mixing with gladioli is *A. ericoides*, known as the Heather-leaf Starwort. It has pretty pointed heather-like leaves and throughout autumn its 3 ft stems are covered in masses of tiny blooms rather like those of the gypsophila. 'Brimstone' bears tiny golden-yellow flowers; 'Delight' bears pure white flowers and 'Ringdove', flowers of rosy-lavender.

Michaelmas daisies, in bloom at the same time as the mid-season and late flowering gladioli may also be used. The early flowering 'Tapestry' and 'Fontaine' with their large blooms of tawny-pink are delightful used with crimson gladioli, whilst 'The Sexton' with its flowers of luminous blue and 'The Bishop' with its dusky plum-coloured flowers provide a striking contrast to the orange, white and yellow gladioli.

An arrangement of great richness may be obtained by the use of the long-stemmed montbretias which, like the gladioli, come into use towards the end of July and continue until October. They are especially attractive where used with the Primulinus gladioli. The pink flowered variety 'E. A. Bowles', which is ideal for using with the dusky red and pink Primulinus gladioli such as 'Strawberry Rival', whilst the new hybrid 'Thalia', with its large blooms of clear golden yellow, is outstanding where used with blue and lavender gladioli such as the Primulinus, 'Stylish'. A display of great beauty may be enjoyed by using the scarlet flowered montbretias 'Red Knight' or 'Sir M. Wilson' with Primulinus gladioli 'Sulphur Gem' or 'White Lady'. Montbretias will remain fresh in water even longer than the gladioli.

The spikes should be arranged in small bowls. One, the Alton bowl, in which there is a grid at the top and another just above the base to make for a more artistic display, is made of waterproofed compressed cardboard and is long lasting and un-breakable. The bowls are excellent for use for competitive flower arrangement and for living-room display. Or small, deep bowls may be used into which is pressed a ball of wire netting into which the stems are fixed. A most delightful effect may be obtained by using spikes of the small type gladioli and the new montbretia hybrids in this way.

The miniature gladioli may also be used with the new pom-pom chrysanthemums the first of which come into bloom at the same time as the earliest of the gladioli, the latest with the late flowering gladioli. These dainty little chrysanthemums bear small double blooms, the size of a shilling on branching stems, and whilst a number are more suited to pot plant culture, growing only 12–15 ins. high, many will grow to a height of 2–2½ ft and lend themselves to cutting to use with small flowering gladioli. Early to bloom is the bright pink flowered pom, 'Jessie Milne', whilst 'Tiny Tim' produces masses of citron-yellow flowers in loose sprays. Lovely, too, for mixing is Christine with its blooms of silvery-lilac and 'Orange Lad', its bright orange-coloured blooms having a striking red centre.

Several of the hardy Korean chrysanthemums which, like the pompom, may be left in the ground throughout winter may also be grown for mixing with gladioli. 'Otley Beauty' with its chestnut-red blooms and 'Amber Gem' both make compact bushes about 20 in. high and come into bloom during August.

Nor must the hardy heleniums be forgotten. Probably the best is 'Wyndley', with its flowers of coppery-orange the size of half-a-crown, 'Crimson Beauty' and the new 'Gold Fox' with its blooms of tawny-orange. Each blooms from late July until October and at a height of only 2½ ft.

Few gardeners realise that the Japanese anemones, which grow between 2–3 ft tall and bloom during early autumn, make valuable cut flowers, for they last well in water and are most attractive for mixing with gladioli.

⫷ 7 ⫸

Gladioli under Glass

〰〰〰〰〰〰〰〰〰〰〰〰〰〰〰〰〰〰〰

FEW GLADIOLUS GROWERS REALISE that the plant does well under glass. Where early bloom is required and there is no greenhouse available, the corms may be planted outdoors in prepared beds where they are covered with cloches or with garden frames. A cold greenhouse will also bear its full quota of bloom in spring.

To bear bloom in a cold, or in a gently warmed greenhouse, two forms of the gladiolus, *G. colvillei* and *G. nanus*, are used. *G. colvillei* has for its parents *G. cardinalis* and *G. tristis*, the latter species having the greater influence on its offspring, for like *G. tristis*, *G. colvillei* grows only about 18 in. tall, the blooms being small and dainty whilst they are spring flowering. The corms require planting in October and only in the south-west is it advisable to do so without giving some form of protection. Even so, in a less mild than average winter, the plants may be disappointing. *G. tristis* may be grown in the same way as *G. colvillei* and *G. nanus*. Its creamy-white flowers have reddish-purple pencillings and possess a delicious fragrance. *G. colvillei* has crimson-purple flowers pencilled with white and there are several named varieties:

THE BRIDE. It is one of the purest of all flowers, both the petals and the anthers being snow-white. It is, therefore, extremely valuable for bouquets during late spring when white flowers are usually scarce. For this reason, the bloom is grown in greenhouses and beneath Ganwick lights, in considerable quantities.

PEACH BLOSSOM. The graceful spikes are of delicate rose-pink, blotched with deeper rose and cream which make the bloom extremely popular with the florist.

SPITFIRE. A magnificent new variety, the blooms are of brilliant salmon-red and are produced with freedom.

Gladiolus nanus follows *G. colvillei* in that it blooms during May and early June, thus almost closing the gap with those large-flowered varieties grown under Ganwick lights or in frames, and which will come into bloom early in July, a month before those which are not protected. With the species of *G. nanus*, the colour of the blooms varies from white through cream, blush pink, to carmine and scarlet, but there are better forms:

AMANDA MAHY. This is perhaps the finest variety of *G. nanus* group, the large, refined blooms being of brilliant orange-scarlet.

ROMANCE. A new introduction of great beauty, the blooms being of a lovely shade of soft salmon-pink with red blotches.

QUEEN WILHELMINA. The blooms, which are of a lovely shade of shell-pink, are produced with freedom.

NYMPH. The blooms are white, blotched with carmine.

ROSE MARY. A new variety bearing bloom of a lovely shade of rose flecked with red.

G. delicatissima is closely allied to the *G. nanus* group. It is also known as the 'Blushing Bride'. It grows to a height of 2 ft and bears larger blooms than *G. nanus*. The blush-coloured flowers are flaked with white and carmine to produce a most colourful effect. It blooms during May and early June.

G. tubergeni is in bloom at the same time. It bears elegant loose spikes above strap-like foliage. The blooms, which are produced on 2 ft stems are of purple-rose and have an attractive white throat. Like the others it is best grown under glass.

G. cuspidatus is also early summer flowering and is a most attractive little species, bearing numerous white flowers flaked with crimson on wiry stems 12 in. in length. It is somewhat hardier than the others and in a sunny corner of the alpine garden will readily increase itself.

G. colvillei may be brought into bloom from the first days of April until early June during which time those corms planted outdoors and covered with Ganwicks will come into bloom. All the early flowering species may be appreciated where obtained in bloom early in the season and as they may be grown in pots outdoors in frames and do not need to be taken inside until February 1st, they are a useful crop to follow early forced tulips and hyacinths. They will occupy the house for only about 12 weeks and then make way for tomatoes. Or they may be grown entirely without heat in the cold greenhouse, though they will not come into bloom until early May when the house may be required for other crops.

Growing in Pots

The corms should be planted in 48-size pots at the end of September or early in October, using two corms to each pot and planting 3 in. deep. They like a compost made up of:

> Sterilised loam, 4 parts
> Well-decayed manure, 1 part
> Silver sand, 1 part
> Lime rubble, 1 part

The materials should be mixed well together and just before the compost is required, 1 oz of superphospate should be mixed into a barrowful of compost. This will encourage root action. Be sure that the manure is thoroughly decayed and where possible obtain cow dung which should be well mixed in with the other ingredients. If animal manure cannot be obtained,

FIG 7—Drying the corms. Excess foliage has been removed.

FIG 8—Gladioli plants tied in small bundles ready for hanging in a warm airy place to dry out.

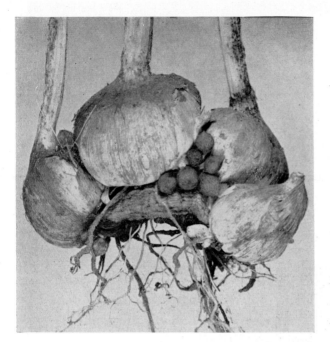

FIG 9—The new corms and cormlets of various sizes.

FIG 10—The old and the new corm and cormlets.

FIG 11—Removing the cormlets to grow on.

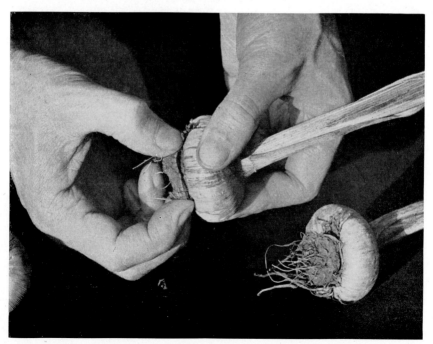

FIG 12—When sufficiently dry, the old corm and roots are carefully twisted away from the new corm.

FIG 13—Using a sharp knife (or secateurs), the stem is severed about an inch above the corm.

FIG 14—Comparative sizes of corms, 12–14 cm, 10–12 cm, 8–10 cm.

use bone meal at the rate of 4 oz to every barrowful of compost. Do not omit the lime rubble, for gladioli are not happy where growing in acid conditions. Where the loam is on the heavy side it will be advisable to mix in a small quantity of moist peat. The compost should be friable and reasonably dry when ready for the pots. Before the compost is added make sure that the pots are well crocked, for efficient drainage is essential. Make the compost quite firm before the corms are planted.

As with all the South African bulbs and corms such as the freesia, ixia and the sparaxis, the gladiolus species should not be placed in plunge beds, for it is important that the foliage grows sturdy from the beginning. After potting the corms, the pots are stood on a layer of ashes in a cold frame, the light being kept in place throughout autumn and winter for again, like the other South African plants, the early flowering gladiolus requires to be kept as dry as possible until it has begun to make growth. No water must be given until the foliage has grown several inches tall which will not usually be until the pots are ready to take indoors.

Make certain that the glass of the frame lights is kept quite clean, otherwise the foliage will grow weakly. The early flowering gladioli require ample light and it is little use attempting to grow them under glass near an industrial city because the pollution of the atmosphere deprives the plants of the necessary light rays, and they will refuse to flower. For this reason, it is never advisable to take the pots indoors until early February when there is a greater intensity of light than during the mid-winter months.

Bringing the Plants into Bloom

The plants may be taken indoors in batches from early February until early March so that there will be a succession of bloom. The pots should be placed as near to the glass as possible. With the forcing-type house they should be allowed to stand on a bench, but with the Dutch light house, which has glass sides, the pots may be placed on the ground.

The plants require a free circulation of air and only very gentle forcing. A temperature of between 50°–55° F. should be provided, but though the appearance of the bloom may be delayed for 7–10 days I prefer to maintain a temperature of between 48°–50° F., for sturdier flower spikes are obtained when temperatures are more moderate. If no heat is available the plants should not be taken indoors until early March, for when once they begin to make growth it is easier to protect them when in the frame by covering with sacking during unduly cold weather. The covering should be removed the moment conditions become milder.

When once the plants are taken indoors and are to be brought into bloom, they should be watered so that the compost is made comfortably moist. It should be kept in this condition until the plants have finished flowering. Never give so much water that the compost remains cold and soggy for any length of time. At all times the moisture should be slowly evaporating so that the roots do not receive more than they can utilise.

As the plants make growth they should be supported by placing two canes or sticks at the side of each pot to enable raffia to be taken around the foliage and tied to each cane. This will prevent the flower spikes from leaning over and growing bent. Or a few 'pea' sticks may be inserted between the foliage as the flower spikes appear.

Alternate feeding with dilute manure water and with soot water each week will greatly enhance the colour and quality of the bloom, and if feeding is continued after the flower spike has been removed and the foliage dies down in summer the new corm will be suitable for using the following season. The pots should be placed outdoors as soon as the blooms have been cut. The spikes are cut as soon as the two lower buds have opened. They are given a long drink before being made up into bunches of six and placed in flower boxes. As the bloom is smaller than that of the summer flowering types, anemone size boxes may be used.

The early flowering gladioli may also be grown in frames, planting the corms in pots any time between early October and early December. The pots should be inserted as deeply as possible into the soil of the frame so that there will be sufficient room for the plants to bloom. Varieties of G. *nanus* which grow no more than 15 in. tall are most suitable for frame culture. The frame should be of sufficient depth to allow for flowering without the spikes touching the glass, but as they come into bloom in May the light may be raised to allow fresh air to enter and this will give additional room for the flowers to develop. The frame lights may be removed entirely on all warm, sunny days, but care should be taken to protect the blooms from being damaged by rain, replacing the lights whenever rain is imminent.

Growing under Cloches

For early bloom, gladioli of the Primulinus and large-flowered type may be grown under Ganwick lights, or cloches; as it is desired to obtain the bloom as early in the season as possible, very early flowering varieties should be grown so that they will provide cut bloom from the end of June until late in July when uncovered plants will come into flower.

As the plants will make rapid growth under cloches and Ganwicks it is not advisable to plant before the first week of March. The ground should be prepared by the trench method, making the bed to the width of the glass covers. Ganwicks are 3 ft 9 in. wide, which will allow the spikes to be cut from both sides without the need to tread the bed.

The method is to take out a trench 3 ft 6 in. wide and 9–10 in. deep and this is prepared as previously described. Fill in the trench to within 3 in. of the top and when the compost has had time to settle down, spread over it a thin layer of peat. Then cover with the Ganwicks about March 1st to enable the soil to warm before the corms are planted. In about a week the corms should be planted 7 in. apart both in the rows and between the rows so that six rows may be planted in the trench. Cover the corms with peat and fill in the trench. Water them in and re-place the glass. If the Double 18 model Ganwick is used this will allow the spikes to reach a height of 18 in. before the glass is removed. If the trench is filled only to 5 in. of the top so that the corms are covered with only 3 in. of soil, this will allow them an extra 2 in. to make growth. The surplus soil may be used for earthing up.

The soil should at all times be kept moist and as the sun gathers strength it will mean that it may be necessary to re-move the glass and give water each day, for the plants will not make early growth if kept dry at the roots. Feeding with dilute manure water and with soot water should be done from the be-ginning of May when the flower spike will have formed in the sheaf of leaves. The plant will then make rapid growth and by the month end the spikes should have reached the top of the glass. By then fear of frost will have vanished and the glass should be removed. To prevent the spikes leaning over, lengths of twine should be taken round the bed, but with close planting the spikes should help to hold each other up. They should be cut as soon as the lower florets begin to show colour.

Ordinary barn-type cloches may also be used to start gladioli into growth. If the corms are planted in trenches filled to within 3 in. of the top, the cloches may be kept in position until the plants have made about 12 in. growth. This they will do by mid-May from a late March planting and the plants will come into bloom by early July, or by mid-June in the more favourable districts.

The following varieties are of compact habit and bloom very

early. They are thus suitable for planting under cloches and Ganwicks:

Large Flowering

Anna Mae	Hokus–Pokus
Aranjuez	Little Pansy
Blue Goddess	Miss Wisconsin
Bow Bells	Myrna Fay
Edith Elliott	Niels Bohr
Friendship	Orchid Lady
Gaylore	Show Girl
Gold Dust	Tahoe

Miniatures

Bonnie Prince	Marionette
Bo–Peep	Pint Size
Corvette	Starlet
Fairy Wand	Toytown
Lavender and Gold	Twinkles
Little Sweetheart	Uranus

⟫ 8 ⟪

Gladioli in Tubs

〜〜〜〜〜〜〜〜〜〜〜〜〜〜〜〜〜〜〜〜

W HERE GARDEN SPACE IS strictly limited, the Primulinus and miniature flowering gladioli, also the less vigorous of the large-flowering varieties, may be grown in tubs. If the tubs are to be used in a courtyard, it is important that they are placed in a sunny position. The plants will revel in the cool, deep root run provided by the tubs and apart from watering during dry weather and an occasional feeding with dilute liquid manure water, they will require the minimum of attention.

The tubs may be used for a succession of bloom, planting them with Cottage and Darwin tulips in early November when the gladioli corms are lifted for storing. At the same time, winter flowering violas and polyanthuses to bloom in spring may be planted around the side of the tubs. These in turn may be removed after flowering to be replaced by trailing lobelia or dwarf geraniums or summer flowering annuals which will prove suitable for planting around the side. The corms will be planted towards the end of March when the tulips will be showing above the surface.

Plant for a succession of bloom by growing together the very early, mid-season and later flowering varieties. In a tub which has a diameter of 2 ft as many as two dozen corms may be planted for no more than $\frac{3}{4}$ in. need be allowed between each corm. It is suggested that three corms each of three early flowering varieties should be planted, selecting them for a pleasing combination of colours. Three corms each of three mid-season varieties and three each of two later varieties would ensure a succession of colour.

The actual size of the tub will be governed by the size of the courtyard or verandah, but the most pleasing display may be obtained from a tub which has a fairly wide diameter and is not too tall. Those most conforming to these dimensions are the cider casks, which are obtainable from most big cider firms. The casks which will have been sawn in two will be of seasoned oak and will not require treating in any way. They will look most attractive where placed against the colour washed walls of house or yard.

Preparation of the Tub

As efficient drainage is essential, holes should be drilled at the base, over which is placed a layer of crocks or broken brick to a depth of 2 in., so that in the event of wet weather, ample drainage is available. Over the crocks should be placed partially decayed turves. The compost should consist of new turf loam, the soil of town gardens which is frequently inert and extremely acid being quite unsuitable. As the compost should be left in the tubs for several years, it goes without saying that it should be well prepared. Kettering loam is excellent where it can be obtained, but loam from pasture land which will be fibrous and free from weed spores will be equally as valuable. Mix with it some well decayed manure, preferably cow manure or a quantity of used hops. Peat is also excellent, especially where the soil is of a heavy nature. A well prepared soil will not only produce a healthy and free flowering plant but will ensure that the plants do not suffer from lack of moisture at the roots. This will enable the tubs to be left for several weeks at a time without the plants coming to any great harm.

Before filling, the tubs should be raised on pieces of wood or crazy paving stone of no more than 1 in. thickness and should be made quite secure so that the tubs cannot tilt. This will greatly prolong the life of the tubs by keeping the base above ground level, providing a circulation of air and preventing the tubs remaining for long periods in pools of rain water.

After the tubs have been filled to the brim with the prepared compost, allow it a full week in which to settle down before planting, when about 2 in. from the soil level to the top of the tub should be left to allow for watering and for a top dressing to be given where necessary.

To prevent the soil from becoming sour, it should be given a top dressing with lime each year when cleared of the summer flowering plants. This, together with the careful preparation of the soil, should give the compost a life of at least four years before refilling is necessary, though a little decayed manure or some hop manure worked into the compost after the gladioli corms have been lifted late in autumn each year will provide additional plant food and moisture retaining humus.

Planting and Care of the Corms

The corms should be planted towards the end of March or early in April but not before the soil is in a suitable condition

after the winter rains and frosts. Use a trowel for planting, settling the corms 3–4 in. deep and making sure that the base of the corm rests firmly on to the bottom of the hole.

After planting the corms, never allow the compost to suffer from lack of moisture or root action will be retarded, possibly with fatal results. The tubs will require little more attention, for annual weeds will be choked out by means of the plants used as a ground cover and where they are not used a layer of peat may be spread over the surface and around the plants when they have made 4 in. of growth. This will also help to conserve moisture.

As soon as the flower can be felt in the sheaf of leaves, feeding once each week with weak liquid manure water may commence and should be continued until the beginning of October so that the new corms and the cormlets will grow as sturdy as possible. After the last corms have flowered, which will possibly be early in October, watering should be withheld so that the corms will be as dry as possible when lifted at the month end. Thus, they will be more easily cleaned and stored.

Where grown in a position sheltered from strong winds, the Primulinus and Miniature flowered varieties should not require staking, though to ensure straight stems the large-flowering varieties should be given support.

Lifting and Storing the Corms

〜〜〜〜〜〜〜〜〜〜〜〜〜〜〜〜〜〜〜

UPON THE SUCCESSFUL LIFTING and storing of the corms depends the quality of next year's flowering spike, and this appertains to all sections of the gladiolus. If the flower stem has been removed with too much foliage the new corms will be deprived of nourishment, and no matter how carefully the corms are lifted and stored the next season's spike will be of greatly inferior quality, and will be quite unsuitable both for exhibition and the top class florist trade. So that a quality bloom may be grown two years hence the new corm should not be allowed to bear a flower, the florets being removed as soon as they appear. In this way the plant is allowed to retain all its foliage to enable it to build up a vigorous new corm to bear a quality bloom the following year. The corm will receive additional help if given regular applications of dilute manure water.

To preserve the vitality of newly formed corms and so that they will bear bloom of exhibition quality the following year, at least five leaves should be allowed to remain on each plant after the spike has been removed. Where growing for garden decoration only the florets will be removed as they fade, and if grown well this will enable the maximum amount of nutrition to be returned to the corm from the leaves and stem.

Corm Production

The growing plants should be fed for several weeks after the bloom has been removed and until the leaves begin to turn yellow. Liquid feeding should then end, for the corms should be as dry as possible when lifted.

A light well-drained soil is better able to produce a disease-free corm than one of a heavy nature, and for this reason everything should be done to bring such a soil into as friable a condition as possible by incorporating ample supplies of drainage materials. A light, sandy soil, will require the addition of humus forming materials capable of maintaining moisture during summer, without which only a small corm will be produced. Few growers are fortunate enough to have a light soil in which to grow their gladioli but where this is so, besides incorporating humus materials, the ground should be given a thorough soaking throughout the summer months whenever the weather is dry. The greatest advantage of a light soil is that autumnal rains will also readily drain away so that the corm may be thoroughly cleaned and dried before storing.

Another reason for growing the early and mid-season varieties is that the foliage will have time to die back before the advent of the autumn rains when the corms should be lifted, whereas with the late flowering varieties the proper functions of the leaves will not be completed before the time is on hand for lifting the corms. The early and mid-season varieties will have finished flowering by the end of August and so the corms will be ready for lifting by mid-October at the latest.

Where growing expensive choice varieties in small beds, it will be advisable to cover them with Ganwicks, or garden lights, as the foliage begins to die down towards the end of September when feeding should be discontinued. This will allow the soil to dry out so that lifting and cleaning will be facilitated. Where covering the beds is not practical, then the corms should be lifted during a period of dry weather in October and if the soil is dry at the beginning of the month, lift without delay. It is just as important to lift the corms before moisture is able to collect about them whilst in a partially dormant state as it is to delay planting in spring until the sun's rays have begun to warm the soil, for excess moisture will not be used up unless there is root activity. During long periods of cold, damp weather and during a particularly wet summer, losses through botrytis may be severe though less so in a well-drained soil than in one of a heavy nature.

Lifting the Corms

There has long been controversy over the accepted hardiness of the gladiolus and in *Amateur Gardening*, there has been much interesting correspondence on the subject. Some growers reported that they had left their corms in the ground throughout the severe winter of 1948-49 without detrimental results. Where the ground is well drained, this is permissible, for with deep planting and by providing a winter covering of peat, decayed strawy manure or bracken, the corms will be adequately protected. In a well-drained soil, the gladiolus is very much hardier than is believed. It is better, however, to play safe and to lift the corms in gardens away from the south coast, though some latitude may be given where the ground is thoroughly drained and the soil is of a sandy nature. Lifting each year permits the detailed inspection of the corms for pests and disease when they may be treated accordingly.

The corms will continue to increase in size for several weeks after they have finished flowering until the leaves begin to die right back, when they will cease to play any part in the future vigour of the corm. The corms should then be lifted without delay. Premature yellowing of the leaves during July, often before the plant has come into bloom, is indicative of Fusarium (see page 92).

Care must also be taken as the corms are lifted to inspect them for Dry Rot Disease, which appears on the corm as small sunken spots coloured black or brown. Always use a small fork for lifting the corms so as not to damage them and take care not to lose the cormlets. Where large numbers of a variety are grown, tie in bunches of not more than twenty otherwise they will not dry quickly.

Drying the Corms

The bunches should be hung up in an open shed, in the same way as for drying onions, and for about two weeks so that surplus soil will dry out and may be readily removed. The less soil adhering to the corms, the more rapidly will they dry and the less liable will they be to disease. As soon as the foliage has become quite dry, during which time the sap will have finished draining into the corms, cut away the leaves about 1 in. above the crown or neck, taking care to ensure that thrips, which may be on the foliage, do not fall on to the corms. The foliage should be burnt at once.

The corms should then be placed in an airy room for three weeks, preferably where a temperature of 60°–70° F. can be maintained. If there is room available on the greenhouse bench this is ideal, provided ample ventilation is given. Wherever the corms are to be dried they must be given ample ventilation, for a warm, stuffy atmosphere lacking a free circulation of air will prevent the rapid drying of the corms which is essential if botrytis is not to gain a hold. If no greenhouse is available, place the corms on trays in a warm cupboard which is left open to enable the moisture from the drying corms to escape. An airy loft or attic may also be used, but it must be remembered that at this time of the year, where natural heat is not so efficient, the corms may take some considerable time to dry and the longer they take the more liable will they be to attack by disease. Wherever the corms are to be dried plenty of fresh air is essential. Corms lifted from light, sandy soil which may have been quite dry when they were harvested will, of course, dry out more rapidly than corms harvested from heavy land which will almost certainly require some heat in their drying.

When dry, portions of the old corms and the old roots should be removed to leave a clean circular scar at the base of the new corms. From here the new fibrous roots will appear when the corms are planted again. The corms should also have the brown husk or outer skin removed, for this will enable the corms to be inspected for disease and at the same time thrips will not be able to hide beneath the husk making them more difficult to eradicate. In a warm, airy room it will take about three weeks to dry the corms.

The cormlets should be removed with care to be placed with any others that might have been removed when the corms were lifted. When thoroughly dry small numbers may be placed in small sweet bags upon which is written the name of the variety. For larger quantities use muslin bags. This is the most suitable method of storing both the cormlets and large corms, though with the latter it will not be practical to store large numbers in this way. Inside the muslin bag is placed a slip of paper containing the name of the variety. The bag is then tied at the top and hung up in a cool airy room. But first the corms should be inspected for disease and if only slightly affected the parts may be cut away with a sharp knife. The cut should then be rubbed with flowers of sulphur. Also both the corms and cormlets should be shaken up in bags containing powdered sulphur. This will prevent an outbreak of botrytis should the storage room not be entirely free from moisture in the atmosphere.

To guard against thrip, which will feed on the corms during storage and cover the areas with a brown cork-like tissue, all corms should be treated either with DDT Lindex or naphthalene before storage. Each preparation should be used at a rate of 1 oz to every ten dozen corms. The corms are treated in the same way as when applying sulphur to prevent botrytis but should not be treated until early November when the chances of thrips entering the storage room from outside will be greatly reduced by the cold weather.

Storing the Corms

The corms should be stored in a temperature which is as near to 50° F. as possible. Frost will, of course, seriously damage the corms and a room free from frost is essential, but where the temperature does not exceed 45° F. there may be some risk of mildew in spite of all precautions. However, should the temperature exceed 60° F., the corms may become too dry and shrivelled, whilst if there are any diseased corms there will be an opportunity of it spreading in too high a temperature. The temperature should be between 45°–55° F., whilst the corms should have a free circulation of air.

If the corms cannot be kept in muslin bags they should be placed in cardboard boxes or in clean wooden trays, but never at any time should they be kept in closed tins or boxes without ventilation and where they will sweat and be liable to botrytis. They should be kept dry and warm, yet they must be prevented from shrivelling, and if stored in a warm room it will be advisable to place the corms in bags (or boxes) of peat. Dry silver sand which, like the peat, will be almost sterile may also be used.

It will be advisable to inspect the corms during the time they are in storage with regularity. Never put them away and forget about them until planting time, for during the five months in storage much can happen. Disease spots which, when the corms were placed into storage, were hardly visible to the naked eye, may after several weeks have spread through the whole corm or may have spread into large areas requiring immediate removal by cutting out with a sharp knife. Again, the atmosphere may be too damp or too dry and by the turn of the year this will be shown upon inspection of the corm which may show signs of sweating or of shrivelling. If steps are taken in time to correct the condition, little or no harm will be done. It will also be advisable to dust the corms again, either with DDT or naphthalene, towards the end of January as a safeguard against thrip having by some way entered the storage room, or against those which may have escaped destruction previously. This is particularly important where large numbers of corms are being stored and it is not practical to remove the husks.

At planting time again inspect each corm, so that any showing signs of disease can be burnt, then either dust again with DDT or immerse the corms in a diluted solution of Lysol (1 tablespoonful to a gallon of water) for three hours. After draining plant the corms at once and whilst they are still damp. And wherever possible to guard against pest and disease, plant on fresh ground at least in alternate years.

FIG 15—Arrangement of 'Leif Erikson'.

FIG 16—Here, gladioli are bordered by violas and interplanted with stocks.

FIG 19—Butterfly gladiolus, 'Spirito'.
FIG 20—Butterfly gladiolus, 'Ice Follie
FIG 21—Butterfly gladiolus, 'Elf'.
FIG 22—Butterfly gladiolus, 'Ares'.

FIG 17—Flower arrangement of Large-
flowered gladioli.

FIG 18—Flower arrangement of Butterfly
gladioli.

FIG 23—Large-flowered gladiolus, 'Cezanne'.

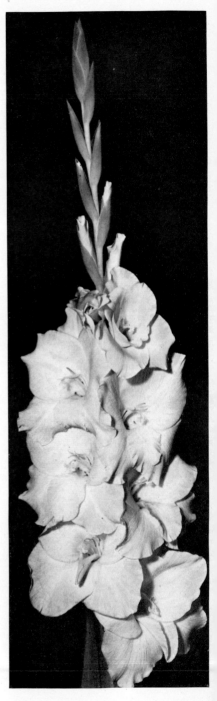

FIG 24—Large-flowered gladiolus, 'Chronique'.

≫ 10 ≪

Raising a Stock from Seed and Cormlets

~~~~~~

W HERE FACILITIES ARE AVAILABLE, the best method of increasing one's stock is either by sowing seed or by growing on the cormlets.

The seed is sown under glass during the first days of March. If deep boxes are used there will be no need to do any transplanting which will not only take up time but which gladioli seem to resent. For sowing the seed use the John Innes Sowing Compost made up as follows:

Per bushel

2 parts sterilised loam
1 part peat
1 part coarse sand
$1\frac{1}{2}$ oz superphosphate of lime
$\frac{1}{4}$ oz chalk

The superphosphate is valuable in promoting vigorous root action, whilst the chalk (or ground limestone) counteracts any acidity of the peat and the gladiolus is never happy in an acid soil.

The John Innes Compost may be obtained from local nurserymen and sundries shops already made up, but the compost should be fresh otherwise the sterilised soil may have become re-contaminated with weed seeds and disease spores, whilst the superphosphate will quickly lose strength.

81

The box should be about 6 in. deep and filled with 4 in. of compost. A large fish box will be ideal. Before filling the box make sure that it is well drained and this is best done by boring holes in the bottom and covering them with crocks. Then provide a $\frac{1}{2}$ in. layer of decayed turf loam to which is added a sprinkling of bone meal and fill up with the compost to within about 2 in. of the top. Make the surface quite level so that all the seeds will receive the same quantity of water and make firm by pressing gently with a square of wood. If dry, water the surface of the compost before sowing the seed.

Sowing the Seed

Seedlings may be raised in the sunny window of a warm room, whilst a garden frame will also be suitable. Indeed, the seeds may well be sown directly into a frame, having first prepared the compost as near as possible to the John Innes formula. As the seedlings resent transplanting they should not be disturbed and so will occupy the frame for a considerable time. It is, therefore, better to sow in boxes.

The seed is small so must be handled with care, the best method being to tip out that which has been saved from each crossing into the palm of one hand and taking a pinch at a time, to scatter this over the surface in the section so named or into its own separate box. When the box has been sown just cover the seed with the dry compost and water lightly. A sheet of clean glass should then be placed over the box to hasten germination.

Where relying entirely on the sun's rays the seed will begin to germinate by the end of April, or early in the month where sown at the beginning of March and a temperature of $55°-60°$ F. is maintained throughout the month. It is important to maintain the compost comfortably moist, but at no time should it be made wet. If moisture is not continually evaporating from the surface then give no water or the seed and the seedlings will damp off. If the box is covered with glass this will help to maintain the compost in a moist condition, but when once the seedlings appear it will be advisable to wipe away each day any moisture from the glass. The glass should be removed entirely when the plants are little more than 1 in. tall and before they reach the glass.

Where there is a cold frame available the boxes should be moved into it early in May when the seedlings, like grass in appearance, are kept growing steadily throughout summer. They should be hardened off in the normal way for half-hardy plants, gradually admitting more air to the plants but protecting them from night frost until the month end when the boxes are allowed to stand out in the open. At all times the seedlings should be watered only when the compost begins to dry out. The compost should be kept comfortably moist and no more, but guard against the compost drying out. The young plants should be kept growing on until early October when they are lifted individually. The foliage will then be turning yellow, whilst they will have formed a tiny corm almost the size of a pea and of the same size as those numerous cormlets to be found clustering around the base of the new corms of flowering size when lifted in autumn.

Those gardening in favourable districts may sow gladioli seed directly into the open ground having first brought the soil to a fine tilth and enriching it with some decayed manure and peat. The seed is sown in drills 1 in. deep and 8 in. apart to permit regular hoeing from the time the seed has germinated. The seedlings are grown on throughout summer keeping them comfortably moist when they should be lifted before the frosts. The seed should not be sown outdoors until early in April when the soil is already becoming warmed by the sun's rays.

Growing of the Cormlets

Not only will cormlets raised from seed take two more years to reach flowering size, so too will those saved from around the base of an established corm and which will be removed when the corms are lifted. Where a stock is raised in this way, the corms will be fully acclimatised to the soil of one's garden and will possess a vigour rarely to be found in older corms. Bloom raised from cormlets grown to their third year will be of a quality unequalled from old corms.

Cormlets are usually to be obtained from specialist growers and saved from modern varieties. As they cost only about a penny each, compared with a shilling each for 12 cm corms, this is an inexpensive way of building up a stock provided one is prepared to wait two years or possibly longer. Quite apart from price the quality of the bloom will be outstanding.

Not all varieties produce the same number of cormlets from an established corm. Some will yield several dozen in a season, whilst others will bear only one or two which are to be found clustering around the base. Again, certain varieties produce 'spawn', which is the term often used for the cormlets (or cormels) which germinate easily, at least 80% growing on to flowering size. With others, no more than 25% will reach flowering size. But all should be given some help with their germination, for in their native haunts they will remain in the ground without ever seeing daylight. Thus they never become hard as they do when lifted and stored over winter.

To start them into growth activities should commence about April 1st. The first thing to do is to soften their hard brown outer shell or covering and this is done by placing the cormlets of each variety in a jar and covering them with a solution of diluted Lysol, made by dissolving 1 tablespoonful to a quart of water. After covering the corms with the solution leave them for 24 hours so that the shell becomes quite soft, whilst the Lysol acts as a safeguard against thrip. The next step is to drain off the solution and to empty the cormlets on to a tray where the shell is removed by pressing between finger and thumb. Then into each jar place a layer of moist cotton wool, sand or peat into which the cormlets are set. The jars should then be placed in a warm cupboard where all light is excluded and there they remain for 10–14 days depending upon the degree of warmth and until they have begun to sprout. The cormlets should then be planted out without delay, mid-April being a suitable time for by then the soil will be warm and the cormlets will grow away at once. Keeping the cormlets in a warm cupboard may be dispensed with, but sprouting them is halfway to success.

The cormlets are planted out in prepared beds. The soil should be light and friable and should have been enriched with a little decayed manure or with some hop manure. Peat should also be used liberally to retain moisture in a sandy soil and to open up a heavy, clay soil. The more thoroughly the soil is prepared the better will the corms grow.

Planting out the Cormlets

They are planted in drills 2 in. deep over a layer of sand. Space the cormlets 3–4 in. apart and allow 12 in. between the drills to permit hoeing. After covering in the drills all that is required is to keep the soil comfortably moist throughout the summer, for the cormlets will not make growth if kept dry. As soon as growth commences keep the hoe moving between the rows to prevent the appearance of weeds and the surface of the soil from 'panning' when the cormlets will be deprived of air. By the time the foliage has died back and the corms are ready for lifting in October, they will be about the size of crocus corms, almost 1 in. in diameter. They should be dried and stored as previously described and the following year should be treated exactly as for fully grown corms, planting them in trenches 4 in. deep and 6 in. apart.

During the second season's growth it will pay to feed the corms with liquid manure each week from the beginning of July so as to build up as large a corm as possible to produce flower spikes the following season. By then the corms will be about 12 cm in size and capable, where grown well, of producing a flower spike of exhibition quality. The corms will be acclimatised to one's soil. If the flower spike is removed during the second season's growth, cutting it off just above the uppermost leaf, the full energies of the plant will go into the building up of a vigorous corm to produce a flower of exhibition quality next year.

Pests and Diseases

~~~~~~

U NFORTUNATELY THE GLADIOLUS IS liable to suffer
attack from several pests and diseases which will cause untold damage to the corms if not checked in time. For this reason
a careful watch should be continually kept for the slightest appearance of trouble, whilst both plant and corm should be given
routine treatment as a means of maintaining the corms in a
healthy condition. Good cultural treatment where the corms
are grown in a well-drained soil and are lifted at the correct
time, together with the careful drying and storing of the corms,
will do much to guard against damage by the numerous
gladioli pests and diseases. Preventative measures should also be
taken to ensure entirely clean corms.

Pests

THRIP (*Taeniothrips gladioli*) This is a tiny black thread-like
insect about one-twentieth of an inch in length which was first
discovered on gladioli in Ohio, U.S.A., in 1930. Since then it
has continued to attack all parts of the gladiolus in all parts of
the world, feeding on the buds, stems, foliage and corms and
causing damage to the plant in all stages of its growth. The
larvae and pupae which are pale yellow in colour are generally
to be found both in the leaf sheaths and in the buds, whilst the
eggs are laid on all parts of the plant.

It takes only 12 days for the adult stage to be reached, the
insects feeding on the corms whilst in storage, though only
rarely will the hard shelled cormlets be attacked. With mature
corms the pests attack mostly the root initials and the buds,

the most succulent parts, covering the corm with a brown tissue.

When the corms have been planted the insects appear above ground with the foliage, feeding on the leaves, stems, buds and flowers. Their presence may be detected by the leaves turning brown, whilst the buds will also turn brown and become dried up. In heavy infestations the flower spike will be stunted whilst the buds will not expand.

The pests are difficult to reach for by daylight they spend most of their time hiding about the leaf sheaths whilst large numbers will often lay their eggs in the leaf tissues. It is, therefore, advisable to treat the leaves individually where growing expensive new varieties and for exhibition. This is done by soaking a small piece of cloth in a solution of Jeyes Fluid, made by dissolving one teaspoonful to half a gallon of water and applying it to both sides of each leaf. The wet cloth should be applied to each leaf in an upwards direction.

From early June the foliage should also be given routine treatment with a suitable spray or powder. DDT or Lindex applied once every 10 days in dust form and to all parts of the plant should keep the plants free from attack. As the pests reach adult form and will begin to lay eggs in 12 days it is advisable to dust every tenth day from early June. An alternative is to use wettable DDT solution or Sybol to spray the plants every tenth day and making quite sure that all parts are covered with the solution. In this respect a fine mist-like spray will prove most effective. Yet another alternative is to make up a solution of 2 oz of Tartar emetic and 8 oz of brown sugar dissolved in 3 gallons of water. This, like all other sprays, should be applied to the foliage early in the season, for should the pests enter the buds they will prove almost impossible to eradicate and will cause considerable damage to the blooms. As soon as the first florets begin to show colour spraying and dusting should be discontinued, though if the treatment has been carried out from early in the season further treatment should not be necessary after the appearance of the first flowers.

An additional precaution against the thrip is to dip the corms in a solution of Lysol or Jeyes Fluid made by dissolving 1 tablespoonful to a gallon of water, prior to planting. The corms should be immersed for 2–3 hours and planted whilst still damp. Some growers use the highly effective Mercuric chloride for treating the corms at planting time, but this is a deadly poison, corrosive to metals and its use should be avoided by those unaccustomed to its handling or where there are children about.

Where planting gladioli in the same ground year after year, treatment of the corms before planting is greatly to be desired, for thrips are able to winter outside in all but the coldest districts when periods of severe frost will kill off the pests. South of a line drawn from Chester to the Wash, either allow the ground at least a year's rest before replanting your corms or treat them according to instructions.

To carry precaution a stage further, dust the corms with DDT upon lifting and again after they have been strung up to die back. Then, after the corms have been dried and before they are placed in storage for winter, shake them up in naphthalene flakes which should be used at the rate of 1 oz to every hundred corms. The flakes, which are harmless both to the corms and to humans, should be allowed to remain about the corms for several weeks when they are shaken off and the corms are replaced in muslin bags where they remain until spring.

With expensive new varieties especially one cannot be too thorough in the treatment of the corms, but those methods suggested should prevent the pest from causing trouble. The old maxim, prevention is better than cure, is, however, most important with gladioli and the control of thrips. It should also be remembered that the vitality of the plants will be seriously weakened by their presence making them liable to attack from various diseases and viruses which will rarely trouble a healthy, vigorous plant. First begin with a healthy stock then protect it in every possible way against its enemies.

WIREWORM A heavy infestation of wireworm, the grub of the click beetle, may cause damage to the corms and roots. The orange-coloured pests of wire-like appearance may sever the newly formed roots at the base of the corm, whilst the pests may also enter the corm itself. Treating the corms with naphthalene flakes whilst in storage will do much to prevent the pests from attacking the corms when planted, but as a further safeguard it will be advisable to treat the soil with Aldrin Dust whilst the ground is being prepared. It should be used at the rate of 1 oz per square yard, or where naphthalene is used for the same purpose it should be used at double the strength.

SLUGS These pests frequently cause damage to the young shoots during spring and during damp weather, whole rows of young shoots may be severed during a single night. No chances should therefore be taken, and as a deterrent it will be advisable to water the ground with liquid Slugit as soon as the young shoots appear. 1 oz of Slugit diluted in 1 gallon of water will be sufficient to treat 10 sq yds of ground. The treatment should be repeated a month later. If the soil is not treated the slugs may lay their eggs beneath the new corms where they hatch out to cause untold damage.

Diseases

DRY ROT (*Sclerotinia gladioli*) With Hard Rot, this is the most troublesome of all gladioli diseases accounting for many losses both during storage and whilst the plants are growing.

The symptoms are first, the yellowing of the leaves which decay near the base of the sheath, finally, falling away altogether. Upon lifting, the new corm will reveal brown markings which later turn black and become sunken. The roots, also, will be infected.

As soon as any yellowing of the leaves is detected the plant should be dug up and destroyed, after inspecting the corm to confirm the presence of the disease. Often, plants may be only slightly infected and will not reveal yellowing of the foliage until late in the season when this may be taken for dying back in the normal way. Upon lifting, one or two brown spots on the corm may go unnoticed until later, when upon close inspection of the corms in storage the spots may have spread. It is, therefore, important to inspect the corms frequently when in storage. Upon opening the corm where just one or two spots are observed, dense brown streaking will confirm one's diagnosis.

The fungus is unable to live in the soil, only on the corm or plant. For this reason it is important to clear the ground thoroughly each autumn of all corms and foliage. Better still it is safer to carry out rotation of crops. Always obtain corms which are entirely clean. A badly drained soil will also encourage the disease, especially where the corms are left too long in the ground, whilst the use of artificial manures, apart from a little sulphate of potash, and the excessive use of rank farmyard manure may also cause trouble. Correct storage is of extreme importance, for in a damp atmosphere the disease will spread rapidly through the corm.

Where it can be done, dipping the corms in a 0·1% of Mercuric chloride before planting has given complete control, but most growers have to rely on good cultivations and clean stock, careful storage and rotational cropping to maintain a healthy stock.

HARD ROT (*Septoria gladioli*) As far as the corm is concerned the symptoms are similar to those caused by Dry Rot. It is above ground that symptoms differ and instead of the foliage turning brown, grey spots appear on the leaves from which spores are given off to be washed into the soil during rainy weather. The disease is more troublesome during a wet summer and rarely affects gladioli grown under cloches. Not until mid-July are the spots to be detected on the foliage and where they appear on only one or two leaves they should be removed at once and burnt.

Should the disease take a hold the plants will die back, and if the corms are dug up and inspected, they will be seen covered with bright brown patches which will appear to be sunken into the corm. As the season advances, the patches turn black, the tiny black bodies or sclerotia becoming attached to the husk of the corm, whilst they may also be observed at the base of the stem. Infected corms and foliage should be destroyed without delay and fresh ground chosen for the corms next season, for the spores are able to survive the winter in the ground and will attack healthy corms the following season.

The disease is carried from one plant to another by splashing caused by heavy rain, so too close planting should be avoided where growing in those areas of heavy rainfall. Prevention always being better than cure, and in this case there is none; routine spraying with Bordeaux Mixture from early June should ensure clean plants provided the corms were clean when planted. This is why it is so important to inspect corms in storage every ten days or so and to remove at once any which are infected.

Bordeaux Mixture is prepared by adding $\frac{1}{2}$ lb copper sulphate and $\frac{1}{2}$ lb hydrated lime to 6 gallons of water and applying to the plants during a showery day. The treatment should be repeated every ten days. Remember that a metal container should never be used when making up Bordeaux Mixture.

Growing the corms in well-drained soil, rapid drying and providing correct storage conditions will do much to prevent an outbreak amongst the corms, whilst dipping in a Mercuric chloride solution before planting will help them to resist the disease.

FUSARIUM YELLOWS (*Fusarium oxysporum*) This disease, also known as Premature Yellowing, is one of the most troublesome of gladioli diseases. It usually appears about mid-July, just before the first blooms open when the leaves of an apparently healthy plant begin to turn yellow. The lavender and purple flowering varieties seem most susceptible, whilst 'Picardy' and its offspring possess a high resistance.

The disease may be readily detected, for the yellowing is confined to that part of the leaf between the veins. As the veins remain green for some considerable time the leaves take on a striped appearance before dying back completely.

The disease enters the corm through the roots and attacks the centre of the corm, killing the roots on its way. If the corm of a striped-leaf plant is opened, it will be found to have turned dark brown, but unless the leaf yellowing reveals the trouble it is difficult to detect in the corms when in storage.

All plants which show premature yellowing of the leaves should be dug up at once and burnt, for if Fusarium is the cause the corm will already be infected. The disease will also remain in the soil for as long as seven years, during which time it is not advisable to plant gladioli in the same ground. To plant in the same place year after year will almost certainly lead to a building up of the disease in the soil, so, where possible, give at least a yearly rest between each planting.

Severely infected corms may not reveal the disease until sometime after they have been in storage. They may then take on what appears to be a mummified appearance which signifies Fusarium Rot. The corm will later turn black and will disintegrate completely when handled.

There is no known cure for the disease, but it may be kept to a minimum by the early removal of infected plants, by giving good cultivations and by careful storage. Rotational cropping will also help.

BOTRYTIS (*Botrytis gladiolorum*) Where growing in areas of heavy rainfall, this may prove to be the most troublesome of all gladiolus diseases. Growing in badly drained soil and delaying the lifting of the corms until late in the year will also be detrimental and will encourage an outbreak of Botrytis amongst the corms in storage.

The disease is usually only troublesome amongst growing plants in a wet season when small brown spots may appear on the leaves and on the flower petals, thereby making the blooms unsaleable or unsuitable for exhibition. The spores are usually given off by the disease as it appears on the blooms, and for this reason dead flowers and any which may show signs of spotting should be removed without delay. Too close planting, thereby depriving the plants of a free circulation of air will encourage the disease, whilst it may also appear on the corms if incorrectly dried, or if stored in an excessively warm, humid atmosphere. Dusting the corms with sulphur or Botrilex will do much to control the disease. Corms which become infected with Botrytis may fail to grow entirely, or the young growth will turn yellow and die back at an early stage.

To sum up. To maintain one's stocks in a vigorous, healthy condition

(*a*) Begin by planting clean stock.
(*b*) Give good cultivations.
(*c*) Store the corms under good conditions.
(*d*) Carry out dusting or spraying as routine.
(*e*) Allow the ground to have a periodic rest from gladioli.

PART II

BRITISH GLADIOLUS SOCIETY

CLASSIFICATION OF THE GLADIOLUS

I *Grandiflorus*. This covers all sections except the Primulinus groups:

   (a) Midget-flowered. The florets not to exceed $1\frac{1}{2}$ in. in diameter.
   (b) Miniature-flowered. The florets must be over $1\frac{1}{2}$ in. but must not exceed $2\frac{1}{2}$ in. in diameter.
   (c) Small-flowered. The florets must be over $2\frac{1}{2}$ in. but must not exceed 4 in. in diameter.
   (d) Medium-flowered. The florets must be over 4 in. but must not exceed 5 in. in diameter.
   (e) Large-flowered. The florets must be over 5 in. but must not exceed 6 in. in diameter.
   (f) Giant-flowered. The florets to be over 6 in. in diameter.

II *Primulinus*. The florets to be hooded and must not exceed 3 in. in diameter and carried on slender stems. (Small-flowered: S.)

III *Primulinus grandiflorus*. The florets to be hooded and over 3 in. in diameter, of similar build to the Primulinus and loosely arranged on wiry stems. (Large-flowered: L.)

AMERICAN CPASSIFICATION

	Size
Miniatures	Florets under $2\frac{1}{2}$ in.
Small	,, $2\frac{1}{2}$ in. to $3\frac{1}{4}$ in.
Medium	,, $3\frac{1}{4}$ in. to $4\frac{3}{8}$ in.
Large	,, $4\frac{1}{2}$ in. to $5\frac{3}{8}$ in.
Largest	,, $5\frac{1}{2}$ in. and larger

Varieties of Gladioli

A description of every main modern variety with flowering time; raiser; country; year of introduction and classification.

(VE) Very Early. (E) Early. (EM) Early mid-season. (M) Mid-season. (ML) Mid-late. (L) Late. (VL) Very Late.

LARGE-FLOWERED

A. B. COUTTS (ML). Coutts. Canada. 1953. 1(d).
The florets of apricot-buff shading to golden yellow in the throat. The elegant flower spikes carry as many as 24 buds, 8 open, 8 showing colour and 8 in bud at the same time.

ABU HASSAN (E). Konijnenburg & Mark. Holland. 1941. 1(d).
A magnificent violet-blue gladiolus, 10 flowers open at the same time, each being perfectly arranged, on a good stem.

ACACIA (M). Buell. U.S.A. 1961. (e).
The huge ruffled florets are of a lovely shade of rose-pink with a lighter throat and carry an attractive fragrance.

ADORABLE (M). Konijnenburg & Mark. Holland. 1951. 1(d).
The sulphur-cream florets are slightly ruffled and have an amber-cream blotch in the throat. When in bud, the blooms have a slight greenish sheen. 8 florets open at one time out of a total of 20 on an extremely strong stem.

ADORATION (E). Klein. U.S.A. 1948. 1(d).
One of the finest of all pink gladioli and flowering early, is excellent for cutting. The salmon-pink florets are beautifully placed along the flower head.

ALBERT SCHWEITZER (M). Konijnenburg & Mark. Holland. 1954. 1(d).
A tall, vigorous variety suitable both for exhibition and border display. The salmon-orange florets deepen to fiery orange at the edges and have a scarlet throat.

ALBION (VL). Palmer. Canada. 1950. 1(e).
One of the very last to bloom and too late for northern gardens. The large florets are of purest white with perfect show placement.

AMERICAN EXPRESS (VE). Hartman. Holland. 1951. 1(e).
Extremely early and excellent for cutting. The medium-sized florets are of golden-yellow, shaded deeper yellow in the throat.

ANDRENA (L). Armstrong. Canada. 1950. 1(e).
An attractive variety for southern gardens. The very ruffled blooms are of

97

a lovely shade of phlox-pink with a golden throat, the florets being arranged in double row placement.

ANNA MAE (VE). Pommert. U.S.A. 1945. 1(d).
One of the very earliest to bloom, bearing pure white blooms and valuable for growing under cloches.

ANNIE AMELIA (M). Bott. Australia. 1949. 1(d).
A tall, vigorous grower opening 10 florets together. The blooms are ruffled and of deepest cream. Ideal for the show bench or garden.

ANTARCTIC (EM). Konijnenburg & Mark. Holland. 1952. 1(e).
Bridges the gap between the early and mid-season varieties. The pure white blooms are of ruffled form, whilst the placement makes it ideal for exhibition.

APPLEBLOSSOM (VE). Fischer. U.S.A. 1956. 1(d).
Likely to become a favourite cut flower variety for besides its earliness, it is a vigorous and easy grower. The florets, which measure almost 5 in. across, are of creamy white, edged with appleblossom pink.

ARANJUEZ (VE). Konijnenburg & Mark. Holland. 1944. 1(d).
Extremely lovely flowers of a very soft orange colouring, shading to apricot down the throat. A strong-growing variety of delicate beauty, it will be admired as a garden plant and as a cut flower.

ARISTOCRAT (M). Salman. Holland. 1948. 1(e).
The florets are of wine-red with a blue sheen and have excellent texture. The tall, elegant spike makes it ideal for exhibition and for the back of the border.

ARTIST (E). Salman. Holland. 1942. 1(e).
It is one of the most beautifully coloured of all gladioli, the pale lilac blooms being veined with white and flecked with purple.

ATHLONE (M). Palmer. Canada. 1943. 1(e).
The florets are of an attractive shade of buff-pink. On a 22-bud spike, 10 will be open at the same time, the straight-edged petals giving it a cool, chaste appearance.

ATLANTIC (M). Blom & Padding. Holland. 1952. 1(e).
Opens more florets at the same time than any other gladioli and so has won many show awards. Colour, rich orange-scarlet. Large florets.

BEAUTY ELF (M). Wilson. U.S.A. 1960. 1(c).
A star gladiolus, the ruffled red florets having a striking golden throat. 12 florets open together in perfect double row placement.

BENARES (ML). Konijnenburg & Mark. Holland. 1949. 1(e).
A most unusual and valuable variety, in colour a beautiful almost even tone of clear dawn pink, showing a sharp crimson tongue against salmon-pink on

two lower petals and with a cyclamen throat.

BENGALEN (E). Konijnenburg & Mark. Holland. 1954. 1(e).

This variety is becoming more popular each year for its florets have exhibition placement and are of a delightful shade of orange-pink with an orange-red blotch on the lower petal.

BENJAMIN BRITTEN (EM). Konijnenburg & Mark. Holland. 1947. 1(d).

A grand cut flower variety, the florets being of a lovely shade of bright mauve-pink. A hardy and easily grown variety.

BERMUDA (ML). Roberts. U.S.A. 1952. 1(e).

A truly wonderful gladioli, the large florets having a leathery texture and extremely ruffled petals. As many as 8 open together, the blooms being of a lovely shade of pale salmon-pink with a white throat.

BERNADOTTE (M). Konijnenburg & Mark. Holland. 1948. 1(e).

Clear white with bright scarlet tongue on three lower petals. Where-ever used as a cut flower its extra-ordinary beauty commands instant admiration. Produces a magnificent spike of ideal stature.

BIRD OF DAWNING (E). Konijnenburg & Mark. Holland. 1958. 1(e).

A most beautiful variety of exhibition quality, the large, pale lemon yellow florets having a green sheen.

BLACK CHERRY (M) Rich. U.S.A. 1948. 1(e).

Of classical form, the colour is glistening black-red. The florets open 8 at a time on tall spikes making it an outstanding exhibition variety.

BLOEMFONTEIN (M). Konijnenburg & Mark. Holland. 1943. 1(e).

The salmon-apricot florets are of exhibition placement and will open 10 at a time.

BLUE GODDESS (EM). Konijnenburg & Mark. Holland. 1953. 1(d).

Of the 20-bud spike, 8 florets will open together. The blooms are of clear medium blue with a deeper blotch on the fall petals.

BLUE SMOKE (M). Rich. U.S.A. 1956. 1(d).

A new variety with florets of a lovely shade of rosy-grey, overlaid blue and having a salmon-pink throat. The florets have attractively ruffled petals.

BOISE BELLE (L). Roberts. U.S.A. 1948. 1(d).

For a decade an exhibition favourite in America, the extremely ruffled florets opening 10 together in ideal placement. The blooms are widely edged with salmon-pink which merges into golden yellow at the throat.

BOW BELLS (VE). Butt. Canada. 1954. 1(d).

Outstanding for exhibition as a cut flower and for garden display and has won every possible award. Its heavily ruffled florets are of a lovely shade of pink with a buff undertone.

BROADWAY MELODY (M). Konijnenburg & Mark. Holland. 1949. 1(e).
A particular favourite, the large florets being of a delightful shade of soft salmon-pink and with an attractive creamy-white throat.

BROWN LULLABY (M). Pazderski. U.S.A. 1956. 1(d).
A unique gladioli with a great show bench future. The blooms are of chocolate-tan with red feathering in the throat and with a silver picotee edge to the petals. As many as 10 florets open together.

BURMA (ML). Palmer. Canada. 1943. 1(e).
A large proportion of the best gladioli are late flowering and this is no exception. The rose-purple florets are extremely ruffled and have perfect placement, up to 10 blooms opening together.

CARDINAL DE JONG (E). Salman. Holland. 1949. 1(e).
A good rich purple, darkly flecked and showing in the throat a splash of white which extends in a pencilling along the tongue and on the fringes of two lower petals. Exceedingly rich in colour and of rare charm.

CARDINAL SPELLMAN (M). Byvoet. Holland. 1946. 1(d).
Light violet-purple, a most distinct and richly-coloured variety with exceptionally beautiful open florets of ideal form, gracefully arranged on a strong stem.

CARIBBEAN (E). Baerman-Fischer. U.S.A. 1957. 1(d).
A hardy and robust variety it will open 10 florets together, the colour being delicate blue with a violet throat.

CARINGA (M). Errey Bros. Australia. 1955. 1(d).
Raised in Australia by the Errey Bros. this new variety has all the good qualities of the modern gladioli. It stands up well to extreme heat and dryness and is most tolerant of rain. It opens 10–12 florets together and which are of pure shell-pink with a yellow throat.

CARNIVAL (M). Butt. Canada. 1947. 1(e).
A truly great variety, the large florets being of vivid scarlet accentuated by the clear icy white throat. The florets are ruffled, 8 being open together.

CASWALLOWN (E). Konijnenburg & Mark. Holland. 1947. 1(e).
A superb variety of unusual colouring, the large florets being of the shade of crushed red currants, free from markings.

CATHERINE (ML). Bott. Australia. 1951. 1(d).
One of the most striking of all varieties. The huge florets are of a lovely shade of orange, streaked with chocolate and having a white throat.

CATHERINE BEATH (L). Coutts. Canada. 1951. 1(d).
An excellent yellow for the late shows. The florets, of which 10 open together, have plain edges and are of a deep golden yellow colour.

CEZANNE (E). Konijnenburg & Mark. Holland. 1958. 1(e).

An outstanding variety, the huge florets being of cherry-red with a cream blotch and having ideal show placement.

CHAMOUNY (M). Baerman. U.S.A. 1938. 1(d).

A fine exhibition and garden variety, whilst the tall ribbon-like spikes make it excellent for cutting. The blooms are of bright cerise-pink with an attractive picotee edge.

CHINA BLUE (E). Fischer. U.S.A. 1961. 1(d).

The huge spikes of 20 buds open 10 together. The soft violet-blue florets are the largest of any 'blue'.

CHINOOK (ML). Lines. U.S.A. 1949. 1(d).

Bears one of the largest spikes of all and opens up to 10 huge florets at one time. The blooms are of a glorious shade of bright salmon.

CHRONIQUE (M). Konijnenburg & Mark. Holland. 1953. 1(e).

It bears a spike of exhibition form, the florets being of salmon-pink.

CIRCE (M). Konijnenburg & Mark. Holland. 1947. 1(e).

Clear glowing tangerine, deep crimson streak behind a light throat, decisive light pencilling down the centre of each petal and numerous precise streaks of crimson against a sharp cream tongue on one lower petal.

CONGO (ML). Lines. U.S.A. 1956. 1(e).

This is a magnificent rich black red, having ruffled florets almost 6 in. across. Of the 20-bud spike between 8 and 10 blooms open together.

CONNECTICUT YANKEE (M). Schenetsky. U.S.A. 1944. 1(d).

It opens 8 florets together which have ideal double row placement. The blooms are of a lovely shade of deep pink with red throat blotches.

CORONA (M). Palmer. Canada. 1940. 1(d).

An exhibition gladioli of distinctive appearance, the large, refined white blooms having a picotee edge of rose-pink.

COTILLION (ML). Butt. Canada. 1948. 1(e).

The large florets possess a leathery texture and are beautifully reflexed being of deepest pink with a lemon yellow throat, with perfect exhibition placement.

COVER GIRL (L). La Salle. U.S.A. 1945. 1(d).

Has for long been a show winner in the U.S.A. but it is a valuable cut flower variety, the spikes being long and thin, the florets plain edged and of a clear soft salmon-pink colouring.

CYMBELINE (M). Palmer. Canada. 1951. 1(d).

A grand cut flower gladiolus, opening a large number of medium-sized florets which are a glorious salmon-pink.

DAISY MAE (ML). Lines. U.S.A. 1945. 1(d).

An attractive variety for cutting though rather late to flower. The refined florets are of a lovely shade of rosy-orange with a cherry-red blotch in the throat.

D'ARTAGAN (M). Konijnenburg & Mark. Holland. 1955. 1(e).

A most beautiful variety with ideal floret placement for exhibition. The florets are of lemon-white, slightly flushed with pink and having a crimson blotch.

DARK BRILLIANCE (M). Puerner. U.S.A. 1958 1(d).

The almost black buds open to florets of deep wine red with a silver picotee edge.

DIAMOND (M). Visser. Holland. 1950. 1(e).

Now firmly established as an exhibition variety for it has ideal floret placement. The blooms are of a lovely shade of apricot-gold.

DIEPPE (M). Hassell. Canada. 1945. 1(d).

A popular exhibition variety in America for it opens 8 florets together, the blooms being ruffled and of brilliant salmon-scarlet.

DIRECTOR (ML). Roberts. U.S.A. 1956. 1(d).

A fine new variety having heavily ruffled florets, as many as 10 opening together on a 22-bud spike. The colour is of an interesting shade of deep raspberry red.

DR FLEMING (E). Salman. Holland. 1946. 1(e).

Clear, rose-pink with shell-pink glow on the tongue of one or two lower petals, turning faintly cream in the throat where there are four touches of crimson; flowers of excellent substance grow on a tall strong stem.

DUSK (M). Fischer. U.S.A. 1955. 1(d).

This is a new smoky of a warm copper colour and which is smokier than most in this section. It has a large white throat.

DUSTY MILLER (ML). Elliott. Canada. 1945. 1(d).

A fine early variety which does well in all weathers and in all soils. 8 florets open together and have excellent placement, the blooms being of a unique shade of smoky old-rose.

DUTCH BEAUTY (EM). Visser. Holland. 1955. 1(e).

A new variety of ideal exhibition placement, the huge blooms being of bright violet with a purple blotch in the throat.

EDITH ELLIOTT (M). Bott. Australia. 1949. 1(d).

A charming variety of dainty habit, the blooms being white, tinged with pale pink. The ruffled petals add to its beauty.

EDNA NUTHALL (M). Salman. Holland. 1952. 1(e).

A first class cut flower variety of recent introduction, the blooms being of a beautiful clear salmon-red colour.

EIFFEL TOWER (M). Bott. Australia. 1948. 1(e).

One of the tallest growing of all, often attaining a height of 6 ft and bearing a 24 bud spike of which a dozen or more florets will open together. The large florets are of bright lavender-pink with a striking white throat.

EILLEN (M). Toon. New Zealand. 1950. 1(e).

Sure to become a firm favourite, it bears a flower head 3 ft in length, 10 florets opening together to make it a grand variety for exhibition. The florets, which measure more than 6 in. across, are of bright coral pink with an orange flush at the throat.

ELIZABETH THE QUEEN (M). White. Canada. 1941. 1(e).

After 'Spic and Span', has won more awards at the American shows than any other variety. The blooms are of purest lavender and beautifully ruffled. 8–10 florets will open together and have excellent placement. Like 'Picardy', has been widely used for breeding during recent years.

ELMER'S ROSE (ML). Fischer. U.S.A. 1951. 1(d).

A variety of great all-round merit, the 20-bud spike opening 10 florets together and which are heavily ruffled. The colour is pure deep rose.

EMPEROR (M). Fischer-Baerman. U.S.A. 1958. 1(d).

On the 3 ft long flower head, 8 florets will open together and are of a rich royal purple colour, edged with white.

ERIDGE (M). Visser. Holland. 1951. 1(d).

An all-blue gladiolus of exceptional merit, the colour being a beautiful even tone of pale mauve-blue, slightly darker in the throat. Produces a medium-sized graceful spike, its nicely formed florets and perfect carriage adding to its beauty and distinction.

EUREKA (L). Salman. Holland. 1953. 1(e).

A magnificent variety, opening 8–10 florets together. The blooms are of an attractive shade of biscuit, flushed with peach pink and with violet streaks in the throat.

EVANGELINE (L). Palmer. Canada. 1948. 1(f).

Though late flowering, one of the most popular. The enormous ruffled florets, which are of a lovely shade of light rose pink, open at least 10 together. Now firmly established as an exhibition variety.

FATA MORGANA (M). Konijnenburg & Mark. Holland. 1952. 1(d).

Bears a spike of great beauty, the medium size florets being of soft shell pink with a yellow throat and have ideal placement.

FIREBRAND (M). Butt. Canada. 1944. 1(d).

A variety of outstanding quality, opening 10 closely packed florets to a flower head. The colour is deep glowing red. A champoinship gladiolus.

FLAMING JET (M). Milton Jack. U.S.A. 1958. 1(d).

On the enormous spikes, 10 ruffled florets will open together and are of purest red with a deep cream throat.

FLORENCE NIGHTINGALE (ML). Harris. Canada. 1947. 1(e).

Not so late as Albion and thus more popular. The tall, graceful spike forms

22 buds of which up to 20 open together. The florets are of purest white with attractively frilled petals and attain enormous size.

FLORIST'S GLORY (M). Burn. New Zealand. 1951. 1(e).
One of the finest of the blue gladioli, the large, beautifully placed florets being of a lovely shade of clear lavender-blue, feathered with dark blue in the throat.

FLOWER DREAM (M). Konijnenburg & Mark. Holland. 1948. 1(d).
The beautifully placed florets are of an attractive shade of bright rosy-salmon.

FLOWER SONG (E). Konijnenburg & Mark. Holland. 1952. 1(e).
The florets possess outstanding texture and open 8 on a 20-bud spike. Placement is ideal for exhibition, whilst the colour is rich pure yellow.

FLYING FORTRESS (L). Wilson. U.S.A. 1943. 1(e).
Forms a large flower head and opens 8 florets together; the colour being smoky lavender with a striking carmine throat.

FRANS HALS (M). Salman. Holland. 1948. 1(d).
Deep rust-orange with a heavy brown fleck and a fringe of violet, against a halo of scarlet on lower petals.

FRIENDSHIP (VE). Fischer. U.S.A. 1949. 1(d).
Besides being one of the first to open its florets is one of the daintiest. The flower heads are of medium size and of an attractive frosty pink colour.

GAYLORE (M). Harris. Canada. 1944. 1(c).
A fine all-round variety of easy culture, the large florets are of pale salmon-pink with a pronounced cream throat.

GEM STATE (L). Roberts. U.S.A. 1955. 1(d).
The florets which are of a combination of pale pink and cream, open as many as 12 together. Placement is ideal.

GENERAL EISENHOWER (ML). Salman. Holland. 1946. 1(e).
A grand all-round gladiolus, the florets possessing great substance and exhibition placement and being of a lovely shade of clear hydrangea pink.

GENGHIS KHAN (M). Scheer. U.S.A. 1950. 1(d).
Excellent for cutting and garden display, the blooms have a leathery texture, the petals being ruffled and of a rich salmon-pink colour.

GEOFF. WIGHTMAN (M). Bott. Australia. 1950. 1(d).
A deep golden self of great beauty; the florets are extremely ruffled and open 8 together in exhibition placement.

GEORGE MAZURE (M). Bott. Australia. 1949. 1(e).
For placement and purity of form this is outstanding. A vigorous grower and a copious drinker; its blooms are of pale pink flushed with lavender.

GIPSY DANCER (M). Fischer. U.S.A. 1960. 1(d).
It forms a tall spike and bears extremely ruffled florets of vivid orange blotched with yellow.

GOLD DUST (E). Pfitzer. Holland. 1933. 1(d).

Golden yellow, many florets open at the same time; magnificent variety, which produces a strong stalk on which the blooms are nicely arranged. Very effective if planted in large groups against a green background.

GOLDEN FICTION (M). Salman. Holland. 1955. 1(d).

A fine show variety, 8 florets opening together. The blooms are of deep golden-yellow with a green flush in the throat.

GOLDEN SHOW (E). Salman. Holland. 1948. 1(d).

A very remarkable variety on account of its perfectly formed spike; most charming golden promrose flowers of dainty colouring. A group against a background of evergreens creates a delightful picture.

GORGEOUS DEB (M). Wilson. U.S.A. 1949. 1(e).

Quite outstanding, the florets being enormous and of excellent placement. Heavily ruffled, the blooms are of rich salmon-pink with a beautiful golden throat.

GRAND MONARCH (L). Salman. Holland. 1944. 1(e).

Very late, but bears an enormous spike of great beauty, the large florets being of a lovely rich shade of purple-red.

GREEN ICE (M). Barker. Canada. 1957. 1(d).

An outstanding novelty, having ruffled florets opening 8 or 9 to a 20-bud spike. The colour is greenish cream, shading deeper at the centre.

GREENLAND (E). Konijnenburg & Mark. 1954. 1(d).

A good early variety, the large frilled cream coloured florets being shaded with green whilst they have ideal placement.

GREY SUMMIT (M). Butt. Canada. 1950. 1(d).

Almost a true grey with just a slight flush of pink in the throat. The smooth textured florets are of medium size which makes this a good cut flower variety.

GUSTAV MAHLER (E). Konijnenburg & Mark. Holland. 1951. 1(d).

A very pretty variety with its long, tapering spike and medium size florets of violet-blue, the lower petals having a white stripe.

HARMONY (M). Bott. Australia. 1952. 1(d).

A grand cut flower gladiolus which transports well and opens well in water. The blooms, which are extremely ruffled, are of a lovely shade of rose-pink with a cream throat.

HAWAII (M). Salman. Holland. 1946. 1(d).

Rich glowing blood-red with a sheen of richer crimson on the tongue of the lower petals. Extremely beautiful and impressive colour, a garden plant of distinction which blooms so well in exposed districts. The petals are attractively edged with white.

HEIRLOOM (M). Klein. U.S.A. 1952. 1(e).
Ranks with Elizabeth the Queen as the best of its colour. It forms a long spike whilst the florets, which are of deep, clear lavender and beautifully ruffled, open more together than any other variety. The florets are amongst the largest of all gladioli.

HENRI DE GREEVE (L). Konijnenburg & Mark. Holland. 1947. 1(e).
This glorious gladiolus may be regarded as the royal representative of this popular family. It bears very large flowers of a warm apricot-orange colour; 7–8 opening at a time, on a tall straight stem.

HOKUS-POKUS (E). Pfitzer. Holland. 1943. 1(d).
A charming little gladioli for cutting, the vivid buttercup-yellow blooms being blotched with chocolate on the fall petal.

HOMERUS (M). Konijnenburg & Mark. Holland. 1954. 1(d).
An excellent smoky of almost brown appearance, the chestnut-salmon blooms being edged with slate whilst they have a chestnut-brown throat.

HUNTRESS (E). Jack. Canada. 1945. 1(e).
A lavender which is well established for it is one of the best of its colour for the early shows. It will open 8 huge blooms together on an 18-bud spike and has excellent placement.

INNOCENCE (EM). Fischer. U.S.A. 1957. 1(d).
The tall spikes reach a height of nearly 6 ft whilst 10 florets will open at the same time. The blooms are of an attractive shade of delicate pink and possess great substance.

IRISH ROSE (M). Butt. Canada. 1957. 1(e).
One of Butt's new Canadian introductions and an entirely new break in colour. The rich salmon-rose blooms have a unique green throat and are nearly 6 in. across.

JACK FALLU (M). Bott. Australia. 1949. 1(d).
A hardy, vigorous variety bearing large ruffled florets of leathery texture. The blooms are of an interesting shade of smoky brownish-red.

JEAN GOLDING (E). Blackler. New Zealand. 1951. 1(e).
Bears a large spike with flowers of glowing apricot-orange and which have attractive ruffled petals.

JOHAN VON KONIJNENBURG (M). Konijnenburg & Mark. Holland. 1945. 1(e).
An older variety of great beauty for exhibition and garden display, the blooms being of a lovely clear russet-orange. It is an easy and vigorous grower.

JUNE DAY (VE). Roberts. U.S.A. 1946. 1(d).
On of the earliest, it makes a grand cut flower and is valuable for exhibition. The florets, which are of an attractive shade of shell-pink, are beautifully ruffled.

KALEIDOSCOPE (M). Pfitzer. Holland. 1952. 1(c).

A vivid jumble of salmon-pink with flecks of purple, deep salmon and vermilion. It has a grace all its own, produces a striking effect in the garden and for indoor display.

KATHLEEN BRAID (M). Bott. Australia. 1953. 1(e).

It is slow to increase but the smoky brown colouring of its bloom is so interesting that it is worthy of including in every collection.

KESTREL (M). Palmer. Canada. 1945. 1(e).

The blooms are of glowing apricot, enchanting under artificial light which, combined with its neat habit, makes this a fine cut flower gladiolus.

KING DAVID (M). Carlson. U.S.A. 1951. 1(e).

One of Carlson's magnificent introductions. The ruffled florets are of deepest purple with a silver picotee edge. 24 buds make up the flower head, 8 of which open together. Double row placement. Ideal for exhibition.

KING SIZE (ML). Hartman. U.S.A. 1953. 1(f).

Well named for the massive spikes reach a height of more than 6 ft. 8 monster florets open together on a 26-bud flower head. The blooms are of pale salmon pink.

KISS OF FIRE (M). Salman. Holland. 1951. 1(e).

10 florets will open together on the long, tapering spike. The florets, which often measure nearly 6 in. across, are of warm, velvety scarlet.

KOSMOS (M). Konijnenburg & Mark. Holland. 1951. 1(e).

Bears an exhibition spike of great beauty, the peach-pink blooms having a white line down the centre of the petals. The florets have excellent placement.

LADRONE (ML). Palmer. Canada. 1947. 1(d).

The florets are of most attractive colouring being of deep salmon shading to scarlet at the tips and with a large yellow blotch. 8 florets of perfect placement, open to a 20-bud flower head.

LANDMARK (M). White. Canada. 1960. 1(e).

Sure to become a show bench favourite for the florets, which are of a glorious shade of creamy-white, open up to 12 together. The spike will carry as many as 24 buds.

LEEUWENHORST. Salman. Holland. 1944. 1(f).

A seedling of Picardy and one of the finest for indoor decoration, for it blooms early, its huge florets being of soft lavender-pink, overlaid with salmon. May be used with almost any other variety.

LEADING LADY (ML). Johnstone. U.S.A. 1942. 1(d).

A sport from 'Picardy' and possessing all its good points. The large florets are of pure creamy-white.

LEIF ERIKSON (M). Konijnenburg & Mark. Holland. 1948. 1(e).

This magnificent cream variety is a great exhibition favourite. On the 5 ft spikes 10 florets will be open together whilst 8 more will be showing colour.

LIFE FLAME (VE). Konijnenburg & Mark. Holland. 1953. 1(d).

The most vivid scarlet gladioli of all. It blooms well under glass.

LIPSTICK (M). Balentine. Canada. 1941. 1(e).

A most attractive gladiolus, 9 to 10 florets opening together on a 22-bud spike. The ruffled petals are of a charming shade of shell-pink, the blooms having great substance.

LITTLE PANSY (E). Fischer. U.S.A. 1960. 1(d).

A most dainty and early flowering variety for cutting; the light blue florets have pansy-purple blotches. 16 buds make up the spike.

LORELEI (L). Visser. Holland. 1954. 1(d).

During the past two years it has an outstanding show record in the U.S.A. The florets, which measure nearly 6 in. across, are of pale cream, shading to deeper cream in the throat.

MABEL VIOLET. Salman. Holland. 1949. 1(c).

Has been a consistent show winner for the past decade, opening 8 huge florets to a flower head. The bright purple blooms have an attractive cream throat.

MANCHU (E). Palmer. Canada. 1945. 1(d).

One of the best of all gladioli, forming a large flower head and opening 8 florets together. The blooms are of deep yellow, flushed with pink, with a heavy red blotch on the lower petals.

MANDALAY (E). Butt. Canada. 1956. 1(d).

A most beautiful smoky. A tall vigorous grower opening 8 huge florets which are of deep rose shaded with brown and edged with grey.

MANSOER (M). Salman. Holland. 1944. 1(e).

An exceptionally beautiful and distinct gladiolus, dark mahogany red with velvet sheen. This very handsome variety possesses all the good qualities one likes to see and may be successfully used for mass effects in beds and borders.

MARIA GORETTI (E). Salman. Holland. 1950. 1(f).

This exceptional variety surpasses all others in form, size and stature. The purity of its whiteness and the perfection of its large blooms give it a charm and beauty combined with stately dignity not possessed by any other.

MARY HOUSLEY (M). Salman. Holland. 1951. 1(d).

A most pretty variety the florets being of medium size and of creamy-white flushed with yellow and with a vermilion blotch in the throat.

MAUREEN GARDNER (M). Preyde. Holland. 1948. 1(e).

Stately, clear grey-white, loosely flecked with purple, an arresting smudge of biscuit lightly dusted with purple on the tongues of two lower petals, magenta throat, violet anthers. A master gladiolus of extreme loveliness.

MAYTIME (E). Fischer-Baerman. U.S.A. 1957. 1(d).

A delightful gladiolus, the ruffled florets are of deep rose-pink with a contrasting white throat. The spike grows 6 ft tall with as many as 10 florets opening together.

MEMORIAL DAY (EM). Salman. Holland. 1948. 1(e).

This outstanding and distinct variety may be regarded as an improved 'Paul Rubens', the colour being cyclamen purple on a smoky underground. Enormous spike with 6 to 8 florets open at the same time, of perfect form and excellent substance.

MERRY WIDOW (EM). De Bruyn. Holland. 1950. 1(e).

A fine exhibition variety, the blooms being large and of a unique shade of purple-mauve with cream blotches on the lower petals.

MID-AMERICA (M). Knierim. U.S.A. 1947. 1(e).

One of the most vigorous forming a 3 ft flower head of 26 buds. The huge florets are of a lovely shade of light red.

MIGHTY MONARCH (L). Butt. Canada. 1946. 1(f).

Like so many gladioli which bear a huge spike, it is very late flowering. It is ideal for the later shows where it can be brought into bloom. The huge florets are of clear deep crimson.

MIGNON (M). Salman. Holland. 1954. 1(d).

Bears a sturdy spike of excellent form, each flower facing forward and held firmly to the stem. Blooms are pinkish mauve, mostly pink at the top of the petals. The tongue has a sword of rich orchid mauve and feathers of a lighter tone, leading into the mauve throat.

MINARET (M). Fischer. U.S.A. 1959. 1(d).

This variety is likely to have a great future both as a cut flower and for exhibition. The blooms are of a lovely shade of deep salmon pink, 8 opening together on a 20-bud spike.

MISS WISCONSIN (E). Kreuger. U.S.A. 1943. 1(d).

Early and reliable grower for the cut flower trade. The florets, 8 of which open together, are an attractive shade of bright rose-pink.

MOONLIGHT GLOW (EM). Jack. Canada. 1957. 1(d).

The blooms are of pale moonlight yellow of beautiful form. The florets, of which 10 open together, have precision and double row placement.

MOTHER FISCHER (EM). Fischer. U.S.A. 1951. 1(d).
One of the best of all the whites, the florets being extremely ruffled and of heavy substance. 8 florets will open together in ideal placement.

MRS J. McKELVIE (L). Bott. Australia. 1952. 1(e).
Like many of Edw. Bott's introductions it blooms late but is a beauty, the florets being large and of a lovely shade of clear orange.

MRS R. ERREY (M). Errey Bros. Australia. 1947. 1(e).
Does best in cool weather. The spikes grow tall with 10 enormous florets opening to each flower head. The blooms are of glowing black-red.

MRS W. COMMEADOW (M). Bott. Australia. 1950. 1(e).
The florets have ruffled, reflexed petals of a lovely shade of buff-orange with a yellow throat which gives it an appearance of apricots.

MYRNA FAY (VE). Lines. Australia. 1946. 1(d).
A valuable lavender-pink for cutting. It forms a neat, compact spike and is of easy culture. One of the first to bloom.

NIELS BOHR (EM). Salman. Holland. 1947. 1(d).
Grand for exhibition and the early shows. The blooms are of rich orange-scarlet and open up to 10 together.

NINETY GRAND (EM). Ward. U.S.A. 1947. 1(d).
A fine cut flower variety, the large, leathery florets being of rich Chinese red, a most distinctive colour.

NOWETA ROSE (M). Fischer. U.S.A. 1950. 1(e).
A vigorous grower and an ideal show variety forming a 24-bud spike of which 12 large florets will open together. The colour is bright rose, shaded with lavender.

OGARITA (L). Wilson. U.S.A. 1942. 1(e).
A tall, graceful variety with large florets which open well when cut, whilst it has also won many awards on the show bench. The blooms are of a lovely shade of deep salmon-pink.

OKLAHOMA (L). Wilson. U.S.A. 1945. 1(d).
Fine for cutting in favourable districts. The medium-sized florets are daintily ruffled and are of a lovely shade of smoky-grey with a white throat.

OPALESCENT (M). Fischer. U.S.A. 1959. 1(d).
The ruffled florets are of an attractive shade of pearly pink, 10 of which will open together in double row placement.

ORANGE KING (E). Alkemade. Holland. 1951. 1(d).
A very noble flower of exceptional texture and refined quality. The wonderful colour is a lovely warm orange with mauve blotch on base petals; the whole plant is of ideal stature.

ORIENTAL PEARL (ML). Carlson. U.S.A. 1946. 1(e).

Raised by Carlson who was also the raiser of 'Spic and Span', this gladiolus is equally fine. It is possibly the finest pure cream variety being a tall grower and having large florets with smooth petals. The placement is above reproach.

PACTOLUS (EM). Konijnenburg & Mark. Holland. 1946. 1(d).

Daffodil yellow with a broad vermilion and deep crimson tongue on two lower petals. Lovely variety of outstanding colour, the beautifully formed florets are well arranged along the slender stem, producing a graceful spike of particular elegance.

PALET (ML). Kooy. Holland. 1950. 1(e).

Has achieved considerable distinction on the show bench during recent years for its huge florets have excellent placement and are of rich glowing scarlet with purple markings in the throat.

PATROL (M). Palmer. Canada. 1946. 1(e).

One of the finest exhibition gladioli on account of its exquisite form; will open as many as a dozen florets together. The colour is rich buff-apricot shading to yellow in the throat. One of the easiest gladioli to bring to perfection.

PAUL BUNNION (M). Melk. U.S.A. 1955. 1(e).

Almost as vigorous as 'King Size', the huge florets are ruffled and attractively recurving. The blooms are of rich salmon pink.

PAUL RUBENS (E). Salman. Holland. 1943. 1(e).

A distinct variety of a very unusual colour; reddish violet with a pronounced smoky underground and carmine-red blotches. Stems and poise are superb, 8–10 flowers open at one time.

PETER PEARS (E). Konijnenburg & Mark. Holland. 1958. 1(c).

An excellent cut flower variety making a tall, straight spike. The shrimp pink frilled florets are marked chestnut in the throat.

PFITZER'S SENSATION (M). Pfitzer. Holland. 1949. 1(e).

Deep violet-blue which surpasses in richness any of the 'blues'. It has no markings on the petals, the huge blooms possessing ideal placement.

PHANTOM BEAUTY (EM). Bastian. U.S.A. 1947. 1(d).

Fine for exhibition for it will open as many as 12 florets at the same time on a 24-bud flower head. The colour is of a lovely shade of dusky, pastel pink.

PHARAOH (M). Higgins. U.S.A. 1950. 1(e).

It comes from California where this outstanding salmon-pink variety has a fine show record. The spikes grow up to 6 ft tall, the florets being large and of excellent placement.

PICARDY (L). Palmer. Canada. 1931. 1(f).

A magnificent gladiolus which produces a strong stalk on which the florets are nicely arranged. A glorious colour, salmon-pink with darker feather on the lower petals. A garden variety of exceptional merit, very showy as a cut flower and a perfect exhibition bloom. Though introduced thirty years ago, it is still widely grown for cutting though it should be confined to southern gardens on account of its lateness. It has been more widely used for breeding than any other variety.

PINK LUSTRE (E). Jack. Canada. 1960. 1(d).

A variety with a great future for the early shows, opening 8 florets together which have excellent placement. The attractively ruffled florets are of shell-pink with a cream throat.

PINNACLE (L). Jack. Canada. 1956. 1(f).

It requires nearly two weeks longer to come into bloom than any other variety. The giant florets, which open 10 together, are of delicate lavender marked with purple in the throat.

POLYNESIA (M). Konijnenburg & Mark. Holland. 1948. 1(e).

A fine pink of exhibition form, the florets being shaded with salmon and yellow in the throat and with ruffled petals. Will open 8–10 florets together in perfect placement.

POPPY DAY (EM). Visser. Holland. 1950. 1(e).

A very choice gladiolus of singular beauty, the colour being radiant scarlet of great intensity with a white line on the lower petal. Produces a large tall spike with 7 to 8 perfectly formed open florets, prettily ruffled and nicely arranged on the strong erect stem.

PRINCESS (M). Larus. U.S.A. 1953. 1(d).

Has won many honours in the U.S.A. The rosy lavender blooms have an attractive cream throat. A strong vigorous grower.

PRINCESS BEATRIX (VL). Roozen. Holland. 1947. 1(e).

Very late flowering or it would be more widely planted. The soft orange-coloured blooms deepen at the edges to fiery chestnut-orange to present a brilliant appearance.

PRUNELLA (M). Stringer. New Zealand. 1951. 1(f).

Its unusual colouring and magnificent form made it Grand Champion the first time exhibited in Australia. The huge florets are of an unusual blending of coral and plum, with a cream throat, whilst they possess a smoky sheen.

PUCCINI (M). Salman. Holland. 1946. 1(e).

Fuchsia-purple, showing a glow of crimson against a glow of violet on the tongues of two lower petals, green throat. Enormous spike of superb quality. A healthy and sturdy grower, well adapted for all garden purposes.

PURPLE SUPREME (ML). Wilson. U.S.A. 1942. 1(d).

A most striking variety for indoor decoration for the large rich purple blooms which open as many as 10 together, having a striking silver edge.

RAVEL (E). Konijnenburg & Mark. Holland. 1943. 1(d).

One of the best blue gladioli yet produced, being pale blue with mauve

FIG 25—Butterfly gladioli have florets about half the size of the Large-flowered gladioli, and have attractive throat markings resembling butterflies.

Fig 26—Gladiolus *colvillei*, 'The Bride'.

Fɪɢ 27—Gladiolus primulinus.

FIG 28—A pleasing arrangement of Small-flowered gladioli.

blotch on lower petals; 6 flowers open at a time which are of good substance and noble form and well placed on a tall erect stem.

R.B. (L) Upton. Canada. 1940. 1(f).

What a pity it opens so late, for the florets are of most unusual colouring, being of bright russet-brown over a rose-red base. The blooms are amongst the largest, opening up to 8 in. across and 8 together on a 20-bud spike.

RED CHARM (M). Butt. Canada. 1939. 1(e).

Introduced in 1939, it has since held its place as an exhibitor's favourite for the quality of the bloom and florets placement is excellent. The blooms are of rich dark red.

REDCOAT (M). Jack. Canada. 1958. 1(d).

This may take over from 'Red Charm' as the most popular of its colour for exhibition. The clear light red blooms are beautifully ruffled and open 8 together, placement being ideal.

REDOWA. (EM). Butt. Canada. 1948. 1(d).

One of Butt's magnificent scarlets, the blooms being free from any shading and more than 5 in. across of which 8 will open together.

RED SIGNAL (M). Butt. Canada. 1954. 1(d).

Words cannot describe the beauty of this lovely variety, intense fiery red, uniform in colour throughout of a purity which is seldom seen in any gladiolus; 7 to 8 flowers open at a time and are gracefully arranged on the rigid stem forming a grand spike of graceful habit.

RHAPSODY IN BLUE (M). Konijnenburg & Mark. Holland. 1951. 1(d).

Probably the best blue turned out by Konijnenburg & Mark of Holland for which colour they are justly famous. The handsome spikes are of exhibition quality, the blooms being of clear light blue.

RHODESIA (M). Salman. Holland. 1951. 1(e).

The reddish-brown bloom with a scarlet blotch in the throat gives an appearance of smoky mahogany. The florets have ideal placement and possess great substance.

ROBERTA RUSSELL (E). Bott. Australia. 1949. 1(c).

Grows 6 ft tall the most vigorous of the early flowering gladioli; the ruffled blooms of great size and fiery red.

ROBERT GODLEY (ML). Burn. New Zealand. 1951. 1(f).

The florets often measure 7 in. across and are of a lovely shade of old rose, with paeony-purple feathering in the throat.

ROSE CHARM (M). Fischer. U.S.A. 1948. 1(d).

A good cut flower, opening its florets well in water. The bright rose colouring of the blooms is most attractive under artificial light.

ROSITA (M). Woods. U.S.A. 1955. 1(d).

A most attractive variety both for cutting and exhibition. The light rose florets have a deeper rose coloured blotch in the throat. The silver edge to the petals and the fine double row placement of the giant florets makes this outstanding in every way.

ROYAL STEWART (EM). Pommert. U.S.A. 1956. 1(d).
A royal variety in every way, the clear red florets have ruffled petals and are of great size and substance. On the enormous flower head as many as 12 florets will open together.

SALMAN'S SENSATION (L). Salman. Holland. 1951. 1(e).
This is a huge Dutch variety suitable for exhibition, the florets being almost 6 in. across and of a lovely dark violet-purple colour.

SALMON QUEEN (EM). Schrenck. Canada. 1955. 1(e).
Sure to become a great favourite, possessing all the qualities of a top class gladiolus. The ruffled florets open 10 together and are of a lovely shade of pure salmon with a white throat.

SALOME (M). Konijnenburg & Mark. Holland. 1951. 1(e).
A smoky of great beauty, the coral-pink blooms, flushed with apricot at the centre, have a grey sheen. The large florets possess excellent placement.

SANS SOUCI (M). Konijnenburg & Mark Holland. 1950. 1(e).
Fiery scarlet-red with a clear yellow streak down the centre of the lower petal; a delightful variety of wonderful charm. Flowers of excellent substance, perfectly set on the tall straight stem.

SENECA (M). Palmer. Canada. 1950. 1(d).
This variety is gradually earning a reputation on the show bench for the blooms are of a lovely shade of medium rose and open 10 together. The medium-sized florets are of excellent double row placement.

SEQUIN (EM). Palmer. Canada. 1949. 1(d).
A splendid gladioli for cutting and garden display. Of easy culture, it bears a spike of medium size with blooms of clear, deep yellow.

SHOW GIRL (VE). Colyn. Holland. 1950. 1(c).
On account of its extreme earliness a valuable cut flower. The brick red blooms, which are only about half the size of the exhibition varieties, have a creamy yellow blotch in the throat.

SIEGLINDE (L). Konijnenburg & Mark. Holland. 1953. 1(d).
From the famous Dutch firm of Konijnenburg & Mark, it would be more widely grown if not so late flowering. The beautifully formed blooms are of soft primrose flushed with salmon at the edges and have a golden throat.

SILHOUETTE (M). Konijnenburg & Mark. Holland. 1942. 1(e).
The large florets are of a most attractive shade of smoky-pink and grey which makes it ideal for cutting but forms rather too short a spike for exhibition.

SINCERITY (M). Errey Bros. Australia. 1948. 1(d).

There are two of the same name, that raised by the Errey Bros. bearing cream coloured florets of great refinement and have a scarlet blotch on the fall petal. As many as 10 florets open together.

SKYMASTER (M). Salman. Holland. 1946. 1(e).

Pale peach-pink with golden yellow shading in the throat, base petal with faint red tinge; an extremely beautiful gladiolus of exquisite and gentle grace with a most glorious hue. For purity of colour and perfection of texture it has no equal.

SMOKY SUNSET (M). Jack. Canada. 1959. 1(e).

This is a large smoky red of great vigour, the blooms being suffused with violet grey. 8 florets open together.

SNOW PRINCESS (M). Pfitzer. Holland. 1936. 1(d).

A white gladiolus, greenish in bud, which distinguishes itself for size and form. Colour, milky white with tinge of green down the throat. Very strong spike, often 2 ft in length bearing up to 20 florets.

SNOW VELVET (M). Fischer. U.S.A. 1956. 1(e).

Well named, for the blooms are of sparkling white, as many as 10 florets opening together. Sure to become popular on the show bench.

SOUTHERN BELLE (E). Fischer. U.S.A. 1952. 1(e).

A most beautiful variety excellent for cutting and exhibition. The blooms are of deep smoky pink covered in a misty blue sheen. The florets are of leathery texture and have first class placement.

SPARKLER (EM). Fischer. U.S.A. 1959. 1(d).

A dainty, gay variety, the florets being of a combination of clear yellow and brilliant red, the heavily ruffled petals producing a charming effect.

SPIC AND SPAN (EM). Carlson. U.S.A. 1946. 1(d).

Raised by Carlson in the U.S.A. where it has been the most consistent show winner for a decade. The 3 ft long flower heads will open 10 florets together. The colour is a bright deep pink with ruffled petals.

SPOTLIGHT (M). Palmer. Canada. 1944. 1(e).

For years it has been a popular show winner. The blooms which have ideal placement are of deepest yellow with a crimson mark in the throat.

SPUN GOLD (VE). Palmer. Canada. 1947. 1(d).

A grand cut flower yellow on account of its earliness. The plain edged petals are free of any shading, the medium-sized florets being beautifully placed.

STAINED GLASS (M). Burns. Australia. 1949. 1(d).

Raised by Burns in Australia, the blooms are of clear amaranth purple, like the coloured glass of a church window. Up to 10 florets open together on the tall spikes.

STORM CLOUD (VE). Butt. Canada. 1944. 1(e).

One of the earliest to bloom, it forms a large spike and opening up to 10 florets together. The enormous blooms are of an attractive shade of smoky salmon with a yellow throat.

STORMY WEATHER (M). Barrett. Canada. 1947. 1(e).

A beautiful smoky bearing a well balanced spike of various shades of salmon, overlaid with grey and with a cream throat.

STRATHNAVER (M). Peattie. New Zealand. 1947. 1(e).

Of massive proportions, it bears 27 buds on a 3 ft 6 in. flower head, 14 florets opening together. The blooms are dazzling white and measure 6 in. across.

SUNSPOT (M). Roberts. U.S.A. 1945. 1(e).

A lovely variety which has won many show honours in America during the past decade. The large ruffled florets are of apricot-buff, feathered with rose-red in the throat. 10 open together in ideal double row placement.

SWEEPSTAKE (M). Butt. Canada. 1952.

A magnificent exhibition variety, the very large florets being of leathery texture and of soft azalea pink, flushed with salmon at the edges.

SWISS FLAG (L). Blom & Padding. Holland. 1952. 1(e).

Produces a huge spike of excellent double row placement. The large florets are of vivid cochineal red with a large white throat to present a most striking picture.

TABARIN (EM). Konijnenburg & Mark. 1950. 1(d).

A most colourful variety, the blooms being large and having excellent placement. They are of a deep shade of biscuit, flecked with orange and scarlet.

TAHOE (VE). Benedict. U.S.A. 1954. 1(d).

Valuable for cutting and the early shows, for it comes into bloom before the end of July. The 10 florets which open together have perfect placement, the colour being cream, lightly shaded with cream at the edges.

TANGLO (M). Arenius. U.S.A. 1954. 1(e).

A magnificent smoky tan. A tall grower which consistently bears flower heads of exhibition form with 8–9 florets opening together.

TEMPTRESS (M). Fairchild. U.S.A. 1956. 1(d).

A consistent winner in America and a most charming variety. The ruffled florets, which open as many as 10 together, are of a lovely shade of shell pink.

THE RAJAH (M). Jack. Canada. 1951. 1(e).

A tall vigorous grower, opening 8 florets together on a 19-bud spike. The colour is reddish-purple without markings.

TOEKANA (VL). Konijnenburg & Mark. Holland. 1946. 1(d).

The latest of all gladioli to open whilst its blooms are almost black, the darkest of all which makes it a unique variety.

Tosto (E). Vink. Holland. 1951. 1(e).

With its well built spike and large well spaced florets of pure vivid scarlet, an excellent variety for the early shows and for cutting.

Tunia's Aristocrat (L). Bott. Australia. 1949. 1(e).

One of Bott's best smokies, the florets having exhibition placement and being of a lovely shade of smoky-brown and slate, feathered red in the throat.

Tunia's Classic (M). Bott. Australia. 1950. 1(d).

Probably the best of all the yellows where grown cool when the rounded florets, opening 10 together, take on a glorious shade of clear glowing yellow.

Tunia's Fancy (ML). Bott. Australia. 1948. 1(e).

With its ruffled blooms of deep salmon, makes an excellent cut flower but should be confined to southern gardens.

Tunia's Highlight (M). Bott. Australia. 1949. 1(e).

A smoky variety of intense colouring, the large florets being marked with orange, blue, rust and chocolate.

Tunia's Radiance (E). Bott. Australia. 1951. 1(d).

A magnificent variety, its blooms being a combination of orange and gold, the florets having perfect placement.

Tunia's Wizard (ML). Bott. Australia. 1948. 1(f).

Another superb late gladiolus and the most vigorous grower with the largest florets. The plants are gross feeders and must be done well. The blooms are like those of 'Jacob's Coat'—smoky slate, brown crimson and yellow.

Uhu (M). Konijnenburg & Mark. Holland. 1941. 1(e).

General effect is of light purple and salmon, freely flecked, but the tongue on one lower petal being deep cream, delicately pencilled with four strokes of crimson, light fawn throat. An extremely attractive and dainty variety, quite apart from any other.

Vagabond Prince (M). Palmer. Canada. 1935. 1(d).

A particular favourite though introduced a quarter of a century ago. The russet-brown blooms have a striking scarlet throat and on a 20-bud spike, 8 florets will open together.

Victory Day (E). Salman. Holland. 1954. 1(e).

With its earliness and long, elegant spike it is an excellent cut flower, the large deep salmon-pink blooms having a small white blotch in the throat.

Violet Dickinson (ML). Barrett. Canada. 1946. 1(d).

The ruffled florets are white veined with violet in the throat. Of dainty habit, it bears a spike of 18 buds, 6 of which open together.

Welcome (VE). Roberts. U.S.A. 1958. 1(d).

The best early scarlet for exhibition. The long tapering spike opens 10 buds together.

WHITE CHALLENGE (VL). Arnett. U.S.A. 1947. 1(d).
A white having a small red mark on the fall petal and bearing a refined bloom often 6 in. across and of top placement.

WHITE GODDESS (EM). Roberts. U.S.A. 1948. 1(e).
Of easy culture and an excellent propagator, it forms a flower head 3 ft in length on which 8 ruffled creamy white florets open together.

WILLIAM HAGEMAN (M). Byvoet. Holland. 1950. 1(d).
Of ideal placement, the florets are of pure deep yellow to make this one of the best of all yellow gladioli.

WINSTON CHURCHILL (M). Salman. Holland. 1950. 1(e).
A wonderful gladiolus of glowing brilliancy, the large flowers are bright blood-red, slightly flecked, of unequalled beauty and perfect formation.

BUTTERFLY

ANECDOTE (M). Klein. U.S.A. 1953 1(c).
The blooms are of glistening primrose yellow with rather deeper yellow fall petals.

ARES (EM). Konijnenburg & Mark. Holland. 1949. 1(c).
Of exhibition form, the pale amber-white blooms have attractive scarlet markings in the throat.

ATTICA (E). Konijnenburg & Mark. Holland. 1949, 1(c).
The salmon-pink florets are flushed with yellow on the fall petals which also have red markings. A fine exhibition variety as 8–9 florets open together.

BIBI (M). Konijnenburg & Mark. Holland. 1954. 1(c).
The blooms are of ivory, overlaid with pink and splashed with carmine.

BOSTON (E). Konijnenburg & Mark. Holland. 1953. 1(c).
Bright cherry-red blooms having deeper coloured blotches on the fall petals.

BUMBLE BOOGIE (M). Konijnenburg & Mark. Holland. 1956 1(c).
In spite of its name a beauty, the petals being extremely frilled and of a warm shade of shrimp-pink with a scarlet blotch.

BUTTERFLY (M). Klein. U.S.A. 1953. 1(c).
A gladiolus of most unusual colouring, the blooms being of an exotic shade of rose-pink, the yellow throat being splashed with red.

CASSANDRA (M). Konijnenburg & Mark. Holland. 1951. 1(c).
A frilled variety, the bright red blooms having an amber blotch on the lower petals.

COQ D'OR (E). Konijnenburg & Mark. Holland. 1952. 1(c).
The apricot florets are flushed with salmon and have a scarlet throat.

CONSTELLATION (M). Klein. U.S.A. 1953. 1(d).
One of the best, the heavily ruffled blooms being of deep salmon-red,

DAILY SKETCH (M). Konijnenburg & Mark. Holland. 1956. 1(c).
A most attractive dainty variety with extremely ruffled petals. The small cream coloured blooms have biscuit coloured blotches on the lower petals.

DESIRÉE (M). Konijnenburg & Mark. Holland. 1954. 1(c).
No gladioli is of richer colouring, the blooms being of vivid terra-cotta with a golden throat and with crimson blotches on the fall petals.

DOLL'S MINUET (M). Konijnenburg & Mark. Holland. 1955. 1(c).
The small, dainty blooms are of salmon-apricot with a scarlet blotch.

DONALD DUCK (E). Konijnenburg & Mark. Holland. 1954. 1(c).
One of the first to bloom, the lemon-yellow blooms have an orange blotch on the falls.

ELF (M). Konijnenburg & Mark. Holland. 1955. 1(c).
The blooms are of purest apricot, the throat being flushed with scarlet.

FEMINA (L). Konijnenburg & Mark. Holland. 1950. 1(c).
One of the later flowering butter-flies, the peach-pink florets with their frilly petals being most attractive.

FROU-FROU (M). Konijnenburg & Mark. Holland. 1954. 1(c).
A pretty variety, the lavender-rose blooms have a yellow throat and faint white lines.

GIPSY LOVE (EM) Konijnenburg & Mark. Holland. 1952. 1(d).
Extremely colourful, the salmon-orange blooms, flushed with scarlet having a chestnut blotch.

GREEN WOODPECKER (M). Konijnen-burg & Mark. Holland. 1956. 1(c).
An outstanding exhibition variety, the cream-ground florets having a deep green tint, offset by wine-red markings.

HAPPY (M). Konijnenburg & Mark. Holland. 1956. 1(c).
The blooms are of light golden-orange with a deep orange blotch.

HERALD (ML). Palmer. Canada. 1954. 1(c).
The heavily ruffled blooms are of deepest yellow flushed with orange and have a red blotch in the throat.

ICE FOLLIES (M). Konijnenburg & Mark. Holland. 1952. 1(c).
Particularly attractive, the beauti-fully ruffled blooms are ivory-white with amber markings in the throat.

ISABEL (M). Konijnenburg & Mark. Holland. 1954. 1(c).
The extremely frilled blooms are of deep salmon, overlaid with orange and having a bronzy-scarlet throat.

JACQUELINE (M). Konijnenburg & Mark. Holland. 1956. 1(c).
A lovely variety, the soft shell-pink blooms having a yellow blotch and with attractively frilled petals.

LADYKILLER (EM). Konijnenburg & Mark. Holland. 1946. 1(c).
Outstanding, the large orange florets having a spot of scarlet in a yellow throat.

LIOSALOTTE (M). Konijnenburg & Mark. Holland. 1956. 1(c).
The shell-pink blooms have pale yellow fall petals.

LITTLE DIAMOND (EM). Konijnenburg & Mark. Holland. 1955. 1(c).
A superb introduction, the dainty deep amber blooms being overlaid reddish-orange and with a large maroon throat.

LITTLE DOLL (EM). Konijnenburg & Mark. Holland. 1951. 1(c).
An attractive variety, the blush-white blooms having a purple blotch on yellow fall petals.

LITTLE SHEBA (EM). Konijnenburg & Mark. Holland. 1954. 1(c).
The handsome florets are of soft lemon yellow with a large red blotch.

MADAME BUTTERFLY (E). Konijnenburg & Mark. Holland. 1954. 1(c).
The florets are small and refined and are of an attractive shade of shell-pink with violet throat markings.

MAGIC CARPET (M). Konijnenburg & Mark. Holland. 1956. 1(c).
Most exquisite, the blooms being pale yellow flushed with apricot, the fall petals being of deeper yellow with a purple blotch.

MECKY (E). Konijnenburg & Mark. Holland. 1958. 1(c).
One of the best, the bright yellow blooms being heavily overlaid with cerise whilst the small, neat florets are extremely frilled.

MELODIE (E). Konijnenburg & Mark. Holland. 1950. 1(c).
A brilliantly coloured variety, the salmon-pink blooms being deeper at the petal edges with a scarlet throat.

MICKEY MOUSE (M). Konijnenburg & Mark. Holland 1954. 1(c).
The blooms are of ivory with an orange blotch on the fall.

MOIRA SHEARER (M). Konijnenburg & Mark. Holland. 1954. 1(d).
A fine new variety, the ivory-white blooms being edged with yellow whilst the fall petals have crimson blotches.

NOLA (M). Konijnenburg & Mark. Holland. 1954. 1(c).
Very richly coloured, the orange-salmon blooms having maroon throat markings. Has won every honour.

QUEEN'S PAGE (E). Konijnenburg & Mark. Holland. 1954. 1(b).
Extremely dainty, the florets being small and frilled and of sulphur-yellow with a crimson blotch.

REMY (M). Konijnenburg & Mark. Holland. 1956. 1(c).
A pleasing variety, the sulphur-yellow blooms having a magenta throat and deeper yellow fall petals.

RENDEZVOUS (E). Konijnenburg & Mark. Holland. 1952. 1(c).
The colour is pure vivid orange-scarlet with a deeper throat.

SOIREE D'ETE (M). Konijnenburg & Mark. Holland. 1953. 1(c).
A most dainty variety, the cream coloured blooms being flushed with delicate pink and having sulphur-yellow fall petals.

SPIRITO (M). Konijnenburg & Mark. Holland. 1956. 1(c).
The florets are of a distinctive shade of cherry-red with deeper red and violet markings in the throat.

SUMMER FAIRY (E). Konijnenburg & Mark. Holland. 1954. 1(c).
One of the finest, the clear salmon-pink blooms have cream fall petals and a maroon throat.

TITIAN (M). Konijnenburg & Mark. Holland. 1952. 1(c).
A beautiful variety, the lemon-yellow blooms being heavily blotched with scarlet.

TOM THUMB (EM).
The small, dainty florets are of scarlet-orange with a bright crimson throat.

TOPOLINO (EM). Konijnenburg & Mark. Holland. 1954. 1(c).
A particular favourite having nicely frilled petals, the golden yellow blooms having a scarlet blotch.

VIOLETTA (EM). Konijnenburg & Mark. Holland. 1950. 1(c).
Most distinct, the claret-coloured blooms being deeper at the edges and in the throat.

VIVALDI (M). Konijnenburg & Mark. Holland. 1950. 1(c).
Glows like a prairie fire; the deep orange blooms have blood-red markings.

WALT DISNEY (M). Konijnenburg & Mark. Holland. 1952. 1(c).
A new variety of merit, the soft lemon-yellow blooms having a large red blotch.

MINIATURE

APEX (M). Visser. Holland. 1955. 1(c).
The blooms are of a lovely shade of brownish-red, the petals being pencilled with gold.

BONNIE PRINCE (EM). Barker. Canada. 1955. 1(b).
The very ruffled well placed florets are of a lovely shade of rose-pink.

BO-PEEP (E). Butt. Canada. 1948. 1(c).
Usually the first of the ruffled miniatures to bloom, the florets being of delicate buff-pink, stippled with red.

CAMELOT (M). Larus. U.S.A. 1958. 1(c).
The miniature in U.S.A. for 1959–60.

Often 10 of its 20 buds open together. The colour is soft-medium pink.

CORMBRA (M). Visser. Holland. 1958. 1(b).
A show variety with ideal double row placement, the light orange blooms being flecked with red.

CORVETTE (E). Butt. Canada. 1956. 1(b).
Opens 10 florets together. The small, dainty florets are of vivid scarlet.

CRINKLETTE (E). Butt. Canada. 1941. 1(c).
The first of Leonard Butt's wonderful ruffled miniatures, the petals being

heavily crinkled and of an attractive shade of orange-pink.

DAINTINESS (E). Butt. Canada. 1953. 1(c).
The petals are extremely ruffled with precise placement, the blooms being white with a cream throat.

DRESDEN (E). Butt. Canada. 1951. 1(c).
The ruffled petals and clear yellow colouring of the bloom present a wax-like appearance.

EMILY'S BIRTHDAY (E). Butt. Canada. 1953. 1(c).
Quite beautiful, its biscuity-salmon florets being flaked with cerise and with a large golden-yellow throat.

FAIRY WAND (VE). Roberts. U.S.A. 1957. 1(c).
A Wedgewood seedling which blooms very early. The soft lavender-blue flowers have a soft yellow throat.

FIFTH AVENUE (M). Hedgecock. U.S.A. 1951. 1(c).
Of perfect form, the blooms are of pure deep crimson-red.

FIGURINE (E). Butt. Canada. 1951. 1(c).
Probably the finest of the ruffled miniatures, for the blooms have perfect double row placement and are of glorious shades of bronze and gold.

GAILY CLAD (ME). Hardy. U.S.A. 1951. 1(c).
Well described, the very ruffled greenish-yellow blooms having a large orange blotch.

GOBLIN (E). Butt. Canada. 1954. 1(c).
Most attractive, the clear pink blooms having a deep golden throat.

GOLDETTE (M). Butt. Canada. 1954. 1(c).
Opens 8 blooms together on a 20-bud spike, the petals being extremely ruffled and of clear rich yellow. An exhibition favourite.

GREMLIN (E). Butt. Canada. 1952. 1(c).
The light rose-red blooms have a white throat, stippled with red and face upwards.

HEART O'GOLD (E). Fischer. U.S.A. 1950. 1(c).
Florets are ruffled but of Primulinus placement, the creamy-white blooms having a striking golden throat.

HELEN OF TROY (M). Visser. Holland. 1956. 1(c).
Heavily frilled, the soft china-pink blooms are stippled with cerise in the throat.

KERRY DANCER (E). Butt. Canada. 1955. 1(c).
The small flowered, ruffled blooms are of brilliant scarlet and have a yellow throat speckled with red.

LAVENDER AND GOLD (E). Baerman. U.S.A. 1943. 1(c).
Always commands top prices on Covent Garden with its pale lavender blooms with their moonlight yellow throat. Though ruffled, the blooms have Primulinus placement.

LITTLE SWEETHEART (E). Fischer. U.S.A. 1948. 1(c).
Most dainty, the icing-pink of the petals shading to pure white in the throat.

MARIONETTE (EM). Butt. Canada. 1949. 1(c).
Almost like a miniature Butterfly, the red blooms with their deep yellow throat having a large plum-coloured blotch on the lower petal. The petal tips are also edged with plum-purple.

MARY ANNE (E). Klein. U.S.A. 1953. 1(c).
Quite unique, the white blooms being edged with rose.

PARFAIT (E). Larus. U.S.A. 1958. 1(c).
Outstanding for exhibition, opening up to 10 florets together. The small, dainty blooms are of rich pure salmon colouring.

PETER PAN (EM). Butt. Canada. 1950. 1(c).
Very frilled and dainty, the soft salmon-pink bloom being flushed with cerise at the edges, and shaded with brown.

PICOTEE (E). Klein. U.S.A. 1955. 1(c).
Most striking in that the creamy-white petals have a crimson-red picotee edge whilst the top petals are flushed with scarlet.

PINNOCHIO (E). Evans. U.S.A. 1940. 1(c).
The heavily ruffled blooms are yellow, streaked with orange-red.

PINT SIZE (E). Evans. U.S.A. 1954. 1(b).
Ideal for the small garden, the tiny lavender blooms with their creamy-white throat opening 8 together on an 18-bud spike.

PIROUETTE (E). Butt. Canada. 1952. 1(c).
The salmon-pink blooms have a cream coloured throat stippled with crimson.

PIXIE (EM). Klein. U.S.A. 1955. 1(c).
The cream coloured blooms are beautifully ruffled and have ideal exhibition placement.

SKALAWAG (E). Butt. Canada. 1953. 1(c).
A beauty, the deep pink blooms having a yellow blotch in the throat.

SMILETTE (EM). Sisson. Canada. 1949. 1(c).
A most attractive variety, the blooms of old rose having cerise-red feathering in the throat.

STARLET (M). Baerman. U.S.A. 1944. 1(c).
With its small, pure white blooms it is just right for bouquets and should be grown by all commercial flower growers.

STATUETTE (E). Butt. Canada. 1950. 1(c).
A beauty, opening 8 blooms together and which are of pale yellow, stippled with rosy-red in the throat. Probably the best exhibition miniature.

TOYTOWN (E). Butt. Canada. 1954. 1(c).
It blooms very early, opening 8 together on an 18-bud spike. The strikingly coloured blooms are scarlet with a yellow throat.

TWINKLES (E). Butt. Canada. 1948. 1(c).
Very heavily ruffled, the orange-scarlet blooms are flushed with pink, the yellow throat being veined with red.

URANUS (E). Visser. Holland. 1958. 1(c).
A rare 'smoky' miniature. The crimson-lake florets, overlaid with grey, have a splash of cream in the throat.

WEDGEWOOD (M). Fischer. U.S.A. 1947. 1(d).
The blooms are of a lovely shade of lavender-pink with a cream throat.

WHITE LACE (M). Fischer. U.S.A. 1951. 1(c).
Intensely ruffled, its pure white blooms provide a striking contrast to the more richly coloured varieties.

ZIG-ZAG (L). Pierce. U.S.A. 1954. 1(c).
The last of the miniatures to bloom, the small florets of red splashed with gold in the throat, have zig-zag placement up the stem.

PRIMULINUS

S. denotes a Small Primulinus II. L. denotes a Large Primulinus III.

ARIA (M) S. Kuhn. U.S.A. 1948.
Outstanding, opening 8 small florals together on a 17-bud spike. The attractive deep pink blooms have a cream throat.

ATOM (M) S. Hedgecock. U.S.A. 1946.
Unique in its colour, the slightly frilled blooms being of orange-scarlet with a cream picotee edge. Healthy stocks are now difficult to obtain.

ATTRACTIE (M) L. Unwin. Gt. Britain. 1954.
One of Unwin's best, the ivory blooms being suffused with coral and with a crimson throat.

AURORA (E) S. Unwin. Gt Britain. 1956.
New and beautiful, the cream coloured blooms being suffused and flaked with salmon.

BROWN ORCHID (M) L. Van Voorhis. U.S.A. 1940.
Six florets will open together on the willowy spikes, the blooms being of a unique shade of brown with a touch of gold in the throat.

CANDY (E) L. Visser. Holland. 1946.
Quite delightful, the apricot blooms being flecked with cream, the lower petals being marked with orange and with a crimson throat.

CAROLINE (M) L. Unwin. Gt. Britain. 1954.
Very lovely, the white blooms being flushed with pink, which deepens at the petal tips.

CHEERFUL (M) L. Unwin. Gt. Britain. 1952.
Lovely under artificial light, the coral-shrimp blooms having a slate-coloured throat.

CHINESE LANTERN (M) S. De Bruyn. Holland. 1954.

The florets are more widely separated than usual and are of vivid flamered with a bright yellow throat.

CHRYSANTHA (M) S. Unwin. Gt. Britain. 1952.

One of the best, the rich golden yellow blooms having a small scarlet marking in the throat.

CITRONELLA (M) S. Visser. Holland. 1940.

One of the most dainty, the pale yellow florets being held on long, slender stems.

COLUMBINE (M) L. Visser. Holland. 1956.

A fine exhibition Prim. Of pink and white colourings, like icing sugar.

DAINTY (M) S. Visser. Holland. 1952.

Gay and colourful, the upper petals being of bright yellow, the lower petals rosy-red.

DAINTY MISS (M) S. Stancer. U.S.A. 1941.

Of neat, compact habit, the pale salmon-pink blooms have a cream-coloured throat.

DAZZLER (M) L. Unwin. Gt. Britain. 1956.

The vivid vermilion-orange blooms have a violet mark in the throat to make this one of the most richly coloured of all varieties.

DESMOND BLAKE (M). S. Unwin. Gt. Britain. 1957.

A fine exhibition variety, the green-ish-yellow florets being lightly flushed with apricot.

FASCINATION (M) L. Unwin. Gt Britain. 1950.

The cerise-pink blooms have a cream throat feathered with scarlet.

FIERY KNIGHT (E) S. Unwin. Gt. Britain. 1952.

A beauty, the orange-red blooms with their deeper glowing throat present a velvet-like appearance.

FIRELIGHT (E) L. Unwin. Gt. Britain. 1954.

The soft salmon-orange blooms have lighter edges and a cream throat.

FLICKER (M) S. Kuhn. U.S.A. 1946.

6 florets open together, the blooms being of a lovely rich medium orange with red markings on a yellow throat.

FOREMOST (E) L. Unwin. Gt. Britain. 1952.

A most beautiful variety, the salmon-orange blooms deepening at the petal tips; the fall petals being of deeper orange, faintly lined with gold.

GILT EDGE (M) L. Kuhn. U.S.A. 1942.

Most distinctive, the light red blooms having a picotee edge of gold.

GOLDIE (E). S. Unwin. Gt. Britain. 1957.

Florets are of rich pure golden-orange.

GRACE (M) S. Unwin. Gt. Britain. 1954.

New and lovely. The soft coral-pink blooms being ribbed with white whilst the fall petals are of golden-yellow.

GUILDHALL (M) L. Visser. Holland. 1955.
6 florets open together in exhibition placement, the blooms being of a lovely shade of clear salmon-pink with a brown mark.

HARMONY (E) S. Unwin. Gt. Britain. 1954.
Most distinctive, the rich cherry-pink blooms being deeper coloured in the throat.

HELIOS (M) S. Unwin. Gt. Britain. 1954.
Most outstanding, the lemon-yellow blooms being flushed with apricot and with a scarlet throat.

HER GRACE (E) L. Byvoet. Holland. 1944.
One of the earliest Prims, the blooms being of a lovely shade of cattleya-purple with a creamy throat.

IVORY QUEEN (E) S. Unwin. Gt. Britain. 1954.
The blooms are of glistening ivory, marked with purple in the throat.

JANET (M) L. Unwin. Gt. Britain. 1950.
The cream blooms are heavily flushed with apricot and have a large yellow throat.

JOE'S MAID (M) S. Unwin. Gt Britain. 1958.
The vivid orange-scarlet blooms are blotched with purple.

JOE'S RIVAL (E). S. Unwin. Gt. Britain. 1958.
The florets are of brick-red with purple throat markings.

J. S. PEACOCK (M) L. Unwin. Gt. Britain. 1957.
Brilliantly coloured, the blooms are of salmon-orange, flecked mahogany and with scarlet markings in the throat.

KATHLEEN FERRIER (M) L. Visser. Holland. 1954.
Possibly the loveliest variety the deep salmon-pink blooms being flushed with orange and rose markings in the throat.

LEMON DROP (E) S. Unwin. Gt. Britain. 1956.
Quite lovely, the lemon-yellow blooms having deeper yellow shading in the throat.

MAID MARION (M) L. Unwin. Gt. Britain. 1956.
One of the best, the soft strawberry-red blooms, shaded deeper in the throat, having a wire edge of white.

MAUREEN JACKSON (M) S. Unwin. Gt. Britain. 1958.
Perfect form, the florets of a lovely shade of primrose-yellow.

MIKADO (M) L. Unwin. Gt. Britain. 1956.
Of unusual colouring, the salmony-biscuit blooms are flaked with slate and marked with red in the throat.

MILKMAID (E) S. Unwin. Gt. Britain. 1954.
Lovely, the creamy-white blooms shaded darker cream in the throat, having slightly waved petals.

NADIA (ML) S. Leffingwell. U.S.A. 1937.
Forms a large spike of 22 buds of which as many as 10 florets will open

together. The light salmon-pink blooms have yellow fall petals.

ORANGE LADY (M) L. Unwin. Gt. Britain. 1955.
The salmon-orange blooms are attractively marked with scarlet in the throat.

ORANGE PRINCE (M) L. Unwin. Gt. Britain. 1955.
A beautiful variety, the blooms being of deepest clear orange with a large golden throat.

OSAGE (EM) L. Brown. U.S.A. 1935.
A show favourite, 6 florets opening together on a 16-bud spike and being nicely spaced. The blooms are of clear bright scarlet.

PAMELA MUMMERY (M) L. Unwin. Gt. Britain. 1955.
Introduced after having first been discarded to become a Gold Vase Winner and one of the most popular of all Prims. The blooms are of a lovely shade of biscuit-salmon with a cream throat and waved petals.

PEASANT MAID (M) S. Kuhn. U.S.A. 1950.
The blooms are of deepest rose-pink with a darker throat, 6 opening together.

PEGASUS (M) S. Visser. Holland. 1954.
The white blooms are heavily flushed with crimson towards the tips of the pointed petals, the fall petals being of contrasting yellow.

PELLETIER D'OISY (E) S. Lemoine. France.
Really unusual, the blooms being of chartreuse green with red marks in the throat, the florets having exhibition placement.

PINK ENCHANTRESS (E). S. Unwin. Gt. Britain. 1958.
One of the best. The blooms are of soft cerise-salmon, flecked with violet in the throat.

PINK WINGS (M). L. Unwin. Gt. Britain. 1955.
Of exhibition form, the florets are of a lovely shade of soft salmon-pink.

PRETTY LADY (E) L. Unwin. Gt. Britain. 1956.
Of neat, compact habit; ivory blooms flushed with salmon at the edges.

PRIMROSE DAME (M) S. Unwin. Gt. Britain. 1955.
The spikes are dainty, the blooms of primrose-yellow with a deeper yellow throat.

QUEEN OF PRIMULINUS (M) L. Visser. Holland.
Most attractive, the outer edges of the petals being apricot, shading through pink to cream at the centre.

RADIO (E) L. Unwin. Gt. Britain. 1955.
The blooms are of soft, clear orange with a golden throat.

RED WINGS (EM) S. Unwin. Gt. Britain. 1955.
The blooms are of an attractive shade of salmon-cerise with deeper throat markings.

RICHARD UNWIN (M) S. Unwin. Gt. Britain. 1954.

A beauty and a Gold Vase Winner. The blooms, which have excellent placement, are of chestnut-crimson with a cream stripe on the fall petals, whilst the petals have a velvety texture.

ROSAMOND (EM) S. Unwin. Gt. Britain. 1954.

Of dainty habit, the blooms are of a lovely shade of rose-pink with a yellow throat.

ROSY MAID (M) S. Unwin. Gt. Britain. 1955.

The deep apricot-salmon blooms with their yellow falls makes this a most attractive variety.

ROSY MORN (M) S. Visser. Holland. 1955.

The spikes are dainty, the florets small and are of a pretty shade of rose-pink with a cream throat.

RUBY (E) S. Kuhn. U.S.A. 1946.

The ruby-red blooms are darker in the throat. 6 florets open together to make this a popular show variety.

SALMON JOY (M) L. Unwin. Gt. Britain. 1957.

It really is a joy, the pure strawberry-pink flowers being edged with white.

SALMON LADY (M) L. Unwin. Gt. Britain. 1955.

The large, refined blooms are of a lovely shade of apricot-salmon, feathered in the throat.

SCARLET KNIGHT (EM) L. Unwin. Gt. Britain. 1955.

The colour is bright brick-red with a dainty cream stripe down the fall petals.

SCARLET MAID (E) S. Unwin. Gt. Britain. 1955.

Most striking in every way, the small, dainty blooms being of vivid scarlet-orange with a deep crimson throat.

SCOTIA (M) L. Visser. Holland. 1953.

The blooms are of an attractive blending of orange, apricot and yellow with orange stippling in the throat.

SILVERSIDES (E) L. Kuhn. U.S.A. 1947.

Quite unique in that the bright rose-coloured blooms have silver reverses and open 6 together.

STRAWBERRY RIVAL (M) S. Unwin. Gt. Britain. 1947.

The blooms are of a lovely shade of soft strawberry-orange, lighter at the edges and deeper in the throat.

STYLISH (EM) L. Visser. Holland. 1954.

A most welcome introduction, the blooms being of a lovely pastel blue with darker markings.

SULPHUR GEM (M) S. Unwin. Gt. Britain. 1954.

A beauty, the greenish-yellow blooms having a crimson throat.

TANGERINE (E) S. Unwin. Gt. Britain. 1958.

Most colourful, the golden-apricot blooms having a vivid scarlet throat.

TOREADOR (M) L. Unwin. Gt. Britain. 1958.
A fine variety with blooms of rich glowing apricot-orange.

TROEF (M) L. Byvoet. Holland. 1951.
Suitable for exhibition, the refined blooms of apricot-orange being marked with gold.

TWEEDLEDEE (M) L. Van Voorhis. U.S.A. 1938.
Most colourful, the blooms being of a suffusion of crimson and gold, the florets having ideal exhibition placement.

URANUS (M) L. Visser. Holland. 1954.
One of the few Primulinus 'smokies'. The smoky crimson blooms are offset by the small cream throat.

VELVET JOY (M) L. Visser. Holland. 1954.
The blooms are of an attractive shade of garnet-red with a velvet-like sheen of purple.

VIOLET MAID (M) S. Unwin. Gt. Britain. 1958.
Most unusual, the reddish-violet blooms having cream edged petals.

WHITE LADY (E) S. Velthuys. Holland. 1926.
Pure white, the florets being dainty and of perfect shape.

WHITE SAILS (EM) L. Unwin. Gt. Britain. 1956.
Lovely for growing with the richer coloured varieties, the blooms being white with a pale yellow throat.

YELLOW SPECIAL (E) L. Visser. Holland. 1950.
A fine bright yellow for cutting and show purposes, 8 florets opening together on a 16-bud spike.

ZONA (E) S. Taylor. U.S.A. 1927.
One of the first Prims, but still good, opening 6–7 florets together in exhibition placement. The deep pink blooms have a yellow throat blotched with red.

FACE-UP

PICCOLO (E). Koerner. U.S.A. 1947. 1(b).
One of the most dainty, the pure white blooms having a red blotch in the throat. The wiry stems make it valuable for indoor flower arrangement.

RED BUTTON (E). Koerner. U.S.A. 1948. 1(c)
The best in this section, the long tapering stems having 20 or more buds. The bright scarlet blooms have attractive grey stamens.

T. E. WILSON (E). Koerner. U.S.A. 1942. 1(a)
The blooms are of rich salmon-pink with a white throat, the florets being scarcely $1\frac{1}{2}$ in. across which makes this the smallest of all gladioli.

WHITE SATIN (M). Koerner. U.S.A. 1(b).
The florets are very small and of glistening white, and turn upwards instead of sideways.

INDEX